YOU GOTTA TAKE MY MONEY!

SIMPLE BUT POWERFUL SALES TECHNIQUES THAT'S BEEN PROVEN TO WORK

NAVEEN SINGH

This handbook is dedicated to the valued customers who have been more than transactions—they've been the heart of my sales journey. Your questions, challenges, and shared experiences have shaped the insights within these pages. May this handbook serve as a testament to the meaningful connections forged in the realm of sales. Thank you for the pleasure of addressing your queries and the privilege of navigating this dynamic landscape together.

Contents

Contents

Foreword

In the ever-evolving landscape of sales, experience has been my greatest teacher. Over the course of more than 13 years, I've traversed diverse sales domains—from inside sales to insurance, garment to franchise, channel to software, and solution to edtech sales. My journey has not been confined to the vibrant markets of India alone; it has spanned the globe through the avenues of inside sales, allowing me to interact with individuals from varied backgrounds, age groups, and genders.

In the realm of sales, every interaction has been a learning experience. From the harmonious exchanges with beautiful souls to the encounters with those who tested my patience, each engagement has contributed to a deeper understanding of the multifaceted dimensions of sales. This book is an attempt to distill the insights gathered along this journey into a simple guide, offering you a roadmap to success in your sales closures.

It's essential to acknowledge that sales is a dynamic field, devoid of one-size-fits-all solutions. In these pages, you'll find principles and strategies that have proven effective for me, but remember, there are no fixed rules in sales. What works in one scenario might need adaptation in another. This book is a tool, not a formula. Take from it what resonates with you, adapt it to your unique context, and let it serve as a companion in your pursuit of success in the dynamic and ever-thriving world of sales.

Best wishes on your sales journey.

- Naveen

Mastering the Art of Appointment Setting: A Strategic Approach for Sales Professionals

Early Stage: Transforming Initial Resistance into Agreement:

1. Customer's Initial Response:

Customer: "Hey, give me a call later."

2. Strategic Response:

Salesperson: "Certainly, when would be a convenient time for you?"

3. Shifting the Dynamic:

In opting for the response, "When should I call you?" the salesperson adeptly assumes control of the conversation, demonstrating a genuine respect for the customer's time and schedule. This approach establishes the groundwork for a more collaborative and mutually beneficial interaction.

Advanced Stages: Navigating Follow-ups with Finesse:

1. Customer's Response:

Customer: "Call me later."

2. Strategic Response:

Salesperson: "Absolutely. What time would suit you best?"

3. Demonstrating Professionalism:

By introducing a touch of professionalism, the salesperson artfully implies a busy schedule with the phrase, "Let me check my calendar." This not only communicates the value of the salesperson's time but also encourages the customer to appreciate the significance of the impending interaction.

Sealing the Appointment: A Step-by-Step Guide:

1. Salesperson's Response:

"I have a scheduled meeting with a client at 3. Could we possibly meet at 3:30 or any time after 5?"

2. Creating a Time Constraint:

The strategic suggestion of specific alternative times serves to create a sense of urgency and commitment, prompting the customer to consider their availability promptly.

3. Encouraging Customer's Input:

'Does either of those times work for you, or would you prefer a different time?" By actively involving the customer in the decision-making process regarding timing, the salesperson fosters a sense of commitment, making the appointment more likely to materialize.

Key Benefits of This Approach:

1. Positioning as a Busy Professional:

The subtle implication of a hectic schedule strategically positions the salesperson as a sought-after professional, reinforcing the perceived value of their time and expertise. This positioning goes beyond a mere claim of busyness; it is a psychological play that establishes a sense of exclusivity around the salesperson's services.

The Psychology Behind Busy Professionals:

Exclusive Appeal: Human nature is wired to desire what is perceived as exclusive or in demand. By subtly conveying a busy schedule, the salesperson taps into this psychology, suggesting that their time is a limited and coveted resource.

Building Trust: The strategic implication of busyness also contributes to building trust. If others are seeking the salesperson's expertise, it implies a level of trustworthiness and competence that the customer might inherently rely upon.

2. Creating a Sense of Urgency:

Offering specific alternative times introduces a compelling time constraint, subtly pressuring the customer to respond promptly and take the appointment seriously.

Creating a sense of urgency goes beyond pushing for immediate action; it's about infusing importance and gravity into the decision-making process.

The Psychology of Urgency:

Triggering Action: Urgency triggers a psychological response that compels individuals to act swiftly. When faced with a limited timeframe, the customer is more likely to make a decision promptly.

Heightened Perceived Value: The urgency factor also elevates the perceived value of the appointment. The customer is more inclined to view the interaction as a valuable opportunity that shouldn't be delayed.

3. Facilitating Customer's Active Involvement:

By involving the customer in the decision-making process regarding timing, the salesperson not only respects their autonomy but also fosters a sense of commitment. This active involvement significantly enhances the likelihood of the appointment materializing.

The art of appointment setting transcends mere scheduling; it involves the delicate balance of respecting the customer's autonomy while fostering a sense of commitment.

The Dynamics of Active Involvement:

Empowering the Customer: Involving the customer in deciding the meeting time empowers them, making the appointment feel like a collaborative decision rather than a dictated schedule.

Commitment and Accountability: Actively involved customers are more likely to honor the commitment they've helped shape. This sense of accountability contributes to the appointment's success.

Positioning as a busy professional, creating a sense of urgency, and facilitating active customer involvement form the triad of appointment-setting mastery. As sales professionals artfully intertwine these strategies, they not only secure appointments but lay the groundwork for meaningful and fruitful interactions. In the ever-evolving landscape of sales, mastering these nuances propels professionals towards a future where each appointment is not just a transaction but a step towards lasting relationships and success.

Mastering the art of appointment setting is a nuanced skill that transcends transactional processes. It is, in essence, an art form involving strategic communication, active engagement, and a genuine commitment to addressing customer needs. By implementing this sophisticated approach, sales professionals can elevate their appointment-setting skills, ensuring not just appointments but also fostering a deeper connection with committed and engaged customers. In the realm of sales, effective appointment setting is undeniably a multifaceted skill that profoundly influences overall success.

CHAPTER TWO

Decoding the Five Types of Buyers

Not all buyers are created equal; understanding the intricacies of buyer psychology is paramount for a successful sales strategy. In this chapter, we delve into the four most common types of buyers and decipher how to effectively communicate value to each.

1. Cheap Buyers: Chasing the Thrill of a Deal

Characteristics:

- Seeks a good price over perceived value.
- Thrives on discounts, bundles, and special offers.
- Finds satisfaction in securing a bargain.

Sales Strategy:

- Structured Offers: Craft deals that appear exceptionally valuable.
- Urgency: Instill a sense of urgency to motivate immediate action.
- Limited Quantity: Emphasize scarcity to drive their motivation.

Sample Communication: "This isn't just a product; it's an opportunity. A limited-time offer that combines unparalleled value with an irresistible price. Act now to secure this exclusive deal before it's gone."
Sample Communication: "Seize this exclusive opportunity—a limited-time offer combining unbeatable value with affordability. Act now to secure this exceptional deal before it's too late."

2. Difficult Buyers: Masters of the Challenge

Characteristics:

- Enjoy a good fight and challenges during the buying process.
- Seemingly unpleasable, no matter the effort exerted.
- The purchase itself may not be their primary interest; they relish making the salesperson's life difficult.

Sales Strategy:

- Efficiency: Allocate time and energy judiciously, as difficult buyers can be resource-draining.
- Clarify Expectations: Set clear boundaries and expectations from the outset.
- Evaluate Long-Term Value: Assess whether the challenges posed by the buyer are worth the long-term effort.

Sample Communication: "I appreciate the thoroughness you bring to the decision-making process. Let's ensure our collaboration is efficient and effective for both parties."

3. Sophisticated Buyers: Value-Driven and Research-Savvy

Characteristics:

- Base their decisions on perceived value rather than price.
- Conduct extensive research before making significant purchases.
- Value their own conclusions and insights.

Sales Strategy:

- Information Provision: Share relevant and in-depth information.
- Professionalism: Assume a consultative approach, avoiding excessive persuasion.
- Allow Autonomy: Let them draw their own conclusions and decisions.

Sample Communication: "I respect your thorough approach to decision-making. Here's comprehensive information to aid your research. Feel free to reach out with any questions as you navigate through the details."

Sample Communication: "Our product excels in these areas, and while it may not do everything, transparency is key. Here are its limitations, helping you make an informed decision."

4. Impulse Buyers: Driven by the Moment

Characteristics:

- Make quick purchasing decisions based on emotions.
- Often influenced by immediate external factors.
- Enthusiastically respond to time-limited offers and promotions.

Sales Strategy:

- Emotional Appeal: Craft messages that resonate emotionally.
- Create Urgency: Leverage limited-time offers to prompt swift action.
- Highlight Benefits: Focus on immediate gratification and benefits.

Sample Communication: "This isn't just a product; it's an experience waiting to unfold. Seize the moment with this exclusive offer, designed to add joy and satisfaction to your life."

5. Affluent Buyers: Selling Luxury and Convenience
Characteristics:

- Value convenience, luxury, and status.
- Make purchases for reasons beyond basic functionality.
- Appreciate personalized and hassle-free experiences.

Sales Strategy:

- Convenience Sells: Emphasize convenience and personalized service.
- Highlight Status: Associate the product with status and exclusivity.
- Quality Over Price: Focus on quality and uniqueness rather than affordability.

Sample Communication: "Our offering is designed for those who appreciate the finer things in life. It's not just a purchase; it's an experience tailored to make your life more luxurious and convenient."

Understanding these buyer personas equips sales professionals with the insights needed to tailor their approaches, ensuring a more personalized and effective engagement with each unique individual.

CHAPTER THREE

Navigating the Dynamic Sales Landscape

In this chapter, readers will explore advanced sales strategies designed to enhance their overall proficiency in revenue generation. The focus will be on adapting traditional sales funnel concepts to align with the dynamic nature of consumer behavior. Through real-world examples, readers can self-learn and apply these principles to their own sales endeavors.

The Adaptive Funnel Concept

Consider a traditional online marketing funnel, much like the one utilized in common sales practices, featuring top, middle, and bottom segments. Now, picture a scenario where a customer's journey doesn't strictly adhere to the conventional linear path. For instance, a potential buyer may deviate from the expected progression, taking detours that aren't immediately apparent.

Example: Imagine a customer who initially engages with your brand through social media, skips the middle-of-the-funnel content, and goes straight to making a purchase. Understanding and adapting to such non-linear journeys will be crucial for optimizing engagement and conversion.

The Detour Principle

Building on the non-linear concept, let's delve into the idea of customer "segwaying." Picture a situation where a customer, instead of following the anticipated path from the top to the bottom of the funnel, takes unexpected detours. These detours can be opportunities for unique and personalized engagement.

Example: A customer starts with initial interest in your product, then diverts to researching competitor offerings before returning to make a purchase. Recognizing and strategically addressing these detours can significantly impact the success of your sales approach.

The Brand-Building Paradox

While the immediate goal is to generate sales, there's an often-overlooked aspect—simultaneous brand-building. Consider the concept of social capital, where building a brand identity becomes an investment with long-term returns. This involves creating a brand that resonates beyond individual transactions.

Example: Think of iconic brands like Apple or Nike. Customers not only buy their products but also align themselves with the brand's values and identity. Balancing immediate sales goals with the creation of a lasting brand presence is a strategic move for sustained success.

Navigating the Evolving Sales Funnel

Consider the traditional funnel model, much like Fred described, where prospects move from awareness to interest, consideration, and finally, conversion. However, in today's dynamic landscape, people don't follow this linear progression anymore.

Let's explore this idea with a trip down memory lane to the direct mail days, a method I used when I just started with my mentor. In those times, running a newspaper ad was a common practice. For those unfamiliar with newspapers, they were pieces of paper with news printed on them.

So, let's say a small ad in the newspaper caught someone's attention. In response, they would call a toll-free number to receive a free report. After reading the report, they would encounter some kind of offer, transitioning from a display ad to direct mail and finally to an offer.

However, in today's social media-dominated era, the landscape has shifted. People no longer follow this structured progression. Here's where the change happens.

Let's imagine John is running an ad about starting an eCommerce business. Now, suppose you, as a potential customer, find it intriguing but decide not to click on it immediately. Instead, you might mull it over, consider the idea, and eventually decide to explore further.

You land on the landing page and find it interesting, but you're not ready to opt-in just yet. You might want to think about it a bit more. Next, you might decide to delve into John's website to learn more about him as a person, gaining insights beyond the immediate topic of the ad.

A Modern Approach to Engagement

This scenario reflects a more modern approach to consumer engagement. Customers may interact with various touchpoints, moving back and forth, before making a decision. It's not a linear process anymore;

it's dynamic and multi-faceted.

So, the question for you is, does your approach align with this evolving consumer behavior? Are you open to the idea that prospects may interact with your content in a non-linear way, exploring different facets of your brand before making a commitment?

The Non-Linear Journey of Consumer Engagement

In today's digital landscape, the journey from awareness to purchase is no longer a linear path. It's a dynamic, bouncing exploration of various touchpoints. Let's break down this modern approach with an example:

Imagine someone comes across an ad about starting an eCommerce business, similar to what Fred is discussing. They find it intriguing but don't immediately click. Instead, they explore different facets at their own pace.

Maybe they check John's LinkedIn profile or look for YouTube videos where he shares insights on eCommerce. They want to understand his philosophy and get a feel for the person behind the ad. This bouncing between platforms is the new norm; it's no longer a linear progression.

Diverse Touchpoints in the Customer Journey

Consider two scenarios:

Scenario 1 : Sparse Online Presence:

John runs an ad, but when the potential customer explores YouTube, there's no content.

They visit the website, only to find limited information.

A search for a podcast yields minimal results.

The customer begins to question John's credibility and the value he offers.

Scenario 2 : Comprehensive Online Presence:

The same potential customer sees John's ad, goes to YouTube, and finds a wealth of valuable content.

They discover John has authored a book on Amazon and decide to invest in it.

After reading the book, they watch more videos on YouTube, gaining confidence in John's expertise.

They connect with John on LinkedIn, seeking personalized insights for their business.

A month later, an ad pops up about John hosting a webinar. Intrigued, they decide to join.

Post-webinar, they learn about a course John offers, and now, having built trust over time, they make a purchase.

Strategic Presence on Multiple Platforms

This example illustrates the importance of being present on various platforms. Consumers want to connect when and how they choose, and you need to be there to facilitate that connection. It's not about dominating all platforms; it's about having entry points for potential customers to connect with you.

The shift in power dynamics is significant. Consumers want to consume content on their terms, just like on Netflix. They want to binge-watch your content, connect when they feel ready, and on the platform of their choice. It's no longer about how a company wants to communicate; it's about how consumers want to consume.

So, the recommendation is clear: be present on multiple platforms, provide diverse entry points for consumers, and build relationships through content. The more entry points you have, the higher the probability that consumers will choose to do business with you.

In essence, it's not a linear journey; it's a bouncing exploration across various touchpoints. Use your social media platforms strategically to build relationships at scale, leveraging the power of technology to engage with hundreds of people simultaneously. In today's digital age, we cannot afford to ignore this paradigm shift.

CHAPTER FOUR

Strategic Sale Closures – Choosing the Right Environment

Closing deals isn't just about the art of persuasion; it's also about choosing the right setting to maximize the chances of success. Let's explore different scenarios and the strategic considerations for each.

Phone Call: Mastering Timing and Comfort

Understanding the Customer's Environment:

Leverage Knowledge:

During previous interactions, customers often share details about their daily routines. This could include information about work hours, daily commute times, and preferred calling times. Utilize this information to tailor your approach.

Consider Factors:

Take into account various factors that influence the customer's availability and receptiveness. Factors such as work hours, daily commute, and personal preferences play a significant role in determining when a customer is likely to be more open to a sales call.

Adapt Your Schedule:

Flexibility is key. Adapt your schedule to align with the customer's convenience. This not only demonstrates a commitment to meeting their needs but also increases the likelihood of a successful interaction.

Strategic Timing:

Optimal Calling Times:

Choose calling times when the customer is more likely to be receptive. Early mornings, lunch breaks, and late evenings are often considered ideal.

During these times, individuals are generally more relaxed and open to engaging in conversations.

Avoid Busy Work Hours:

Be mindful of the customer's work hours and avoid calling during peak busy times. Interrupting a customer in the midst of a hectic workday may lead to frustration and hinder the effectiveness of the call.

Creating Comfort:

Ensure a Quiet Environment:

Clear communication is paramount. Ensure that your environment is quiet, free from distractions, and conducive to a focused conversation. Background noise or interruptions can detract from the professionalism of the call.

Make the Customer Feel at Ease:

Choose a time when the customer is likely to be more relaxed. A comfortable customer is more receptive to your message. Consider factors such as their daily routine and personal preferences to create an environment where they feel at ease.

Respect Their Schedule:

Demonstrate professionalism and consideration by respecting the customer's schedule. Avoid pushing for a call at a time that may be inconvenient for them. This not only shows respect but also establishes a foundation of trust.

Mastering the art of phone calls involves a nuanced understanding of timing and creating a comfortable environment for the customer. By leveraging knowledge about their daily routine, considering factors that influence their availability, and adapting your schedule accordingly, you can strategically optimize the timing of your calls. Choosing optimal calling times and ensuring a quiet environment demonstrates professionalism and enhances the likelihood of a successful interaction.

In-Person Meeting: Tailoring Locations to Context

On-Site (Real Estate Deals):

Choose the Property Site:

For real estate deals, the location of the meeting holds immense significance. Opting to meet at the property site allows the customer to experience the space firsthand. This provides a tangible and immersive understanding of the property, fostering a deeper connection.

Allow Customer Experience:

An on-site meeting allows customers to explore the property, envision themselves in the space, and assess its unique features. This hands-on experience goes beyond words and images, creating a more vivid and memorable impression.

Address Concerns and Highlight Unique Selling Points:

Being physically present at the property enables the sales professional to address any concerns immediately. Simultaneously, they can highlight the property's unique selling points, emphasizing its value and aligning it with the customer's needs.

At Home with the Family:

Establish a Personal Connection:

Meeting at the customer's home goes beyond the transactional and establishes a more personal connection. It shows a genuine interest in their environment and contributes to building trust.

Show Respect for Time and Environment:

Choosing to meet at the customer's home demonstrates respect for their time and environment. It eliminates the need for them to travel, making the meeting more convenient and comfortable.

Ensure Family Participation:

For contexts where family decisions are involved, meeting at home provides an opportunity for the entire family to participate in the decision-making process. This inclusive approach fosters a sense of unity and ensures that all stakeholders are actively engaged.

In a Professional Setting: Meeting Rooms and Offices

Meeting Room:

Ideal for Formal Presentations and Negotiations:

Meeting rooms provide a controlled and structured environment, making them ideal for formal presentations and negotiations. The setting encourages focus and attention, allowing both parties to engage in serious discussions with minimal distractions.

Create a Professional Atmosphere:

The formal ambiance of a meeting room contributes to a professional atmosphere. This setting sets the tone for a business-oriented discussion, signaling to the customer that the interaction is serious and significant.

Have All Necessary Materials Prepared:

To maximize the effectiveness of a meeting room setting, ensure that all necessary materials and documents are prepared in advance. A well-organized presentation enhances professionalism and reflects a commitment to a seamless and productive interaction.

Office Setting:

Visit the Customer's Workplace:

Taking the meeting to the customer's workplace provides valuable insights into their professional environment. This firsthand experience allows you to understand the culture, dynamics, and unique aspects of their business.

Build Rapport with Colleagues:

In an office setting, you have the opportunity to interact with the customer's colleagues. Building rapport with key stakeholders beyond your primary contact can strengthen your relationship with the customer and contribute to a more collaborative business partnership.

Gauge Business Priorities:

Being physically present in the customer's office allows you to observe the work environment and gain insights into their business priorities. This understanding enables you to tailor your proposal to align more closely with their organizational goals and challenges.

Choosing between meeting rooms and office settings in a professional context involves a thoughtful evaluation of the specific goals and dynamics of the interaction. Meeting rooms are well-suited for formal presentations and negotiations, providing a controlled environment for serious discussions. On the other hand, visiting the customer's workplace offers the advantage of understanding their professional environment, building rapport with colleagues, and gaining insights into their business priorities.

Sales professionals, equipped with the knowledge of when to opt for a meeting room or an office setting, can strategically enhance the impact of their interactions. By aligning the choice of location with the nature of the discussion and the customer's preferences, professionals can create a conducive environment for successful negotiations and foster long-term business relationships.

Luxury Surroundings: 5-Star Hotel Lobby and Restaurants

5-Star Hotel Lobby:

Choose Upscale Locations for Exclusivity:

Opting for a 5-star hotel lobby immediately sets the stage for exclusivity. The lavish surroundings and impeccable service contribute to an atmosphere of sophistication, signaling that the business deal at hand is of significant value.

Create a Luxurious Ambiance:

The ambiance of a 5-star hotel lobby exudes luxury. From elegant furnishings to impeccable decor, these settings are carefully curated to provide a sense of opulence. This creates a backdrop that aligns with the high-value nature of the business being discussed.

Showcase Commitment to a Premium Experience:

Selecting a 5-star hotel lobby for business meetings showcases your commitment to providing a premium experience. It sends a message to your clients or partners that you value their time and engagement, further reinforcing the importance of the collaboration.

Restaurant Meetings:

Opt for Quiet, Upscale Restaurants:

Choosing upscale restaurants for business meetings combines the pleasure of fine dining with the convenience of a professional setting. Opt for quiet establishments with a sophisticated atmosphere, allowing for a comfortable yet private environment.

Use the Relaxed Setting for Personal Connection:

The relaxed setting of upscale restaurants provides an opportunity to foster a more personal connection. The informal nature of dining allows for natural conversations to unfold, creating an atmosphere conducive to building rapport and strengthening business relationships.

Discuss Business in a Comfortable yet Professional Environment:

Luxury restaurants strike a balance between comfort and professionalism. This setting enables discussions to flow smoothly in a comfortable and aesthetically pleasing environment, ensuring that business matters are addressed with a touch of refinement.

Incorporating luxury surroundings such as 5-star hotel lobbies and upscale restaurants into business interactions can significantly impact the perception of the deal and the relationships involved. These environments go beyond mere aesthetics; they convey exclusivity, create a luxurious ambiance, and showcase a commitment to providing a premium experience.

Understanding the nuances of when to choose a 5-star hotel lobby or an upscale restaurant involves considering the nature of the business, the preferences of the parties involved, and the desired atmosphere for the meeting. By strategically leveraging these luxurious settings, professionals can elevate the overall experience of high-value business interactions, leaving a lasting impression of sophistication and exclusivity.

On the Move: Closing Deals on a Plane

Meetings on a Plane:

Consider Private Jet Travel for High-Profile Clients:

For high-profile clients or crucial business discussions, consider private jet travel. This exclusive mode of transportation not only adds a touch of luxury but also provides a confidential and controlled environment for sensitive negotiations.

Utilize Travel Time for Discussions:

In-flight time can be a valuable resource for uninterrupted discussions. Use this time strategically to delve into important details, address concerns, and finalize the finer points of a deal. The confined space of a plane allows for focused conversations without external interruptions.

Ensure a Distraction-Free Environment:

A plane offers a unique environment where distractions are minimized. With limited connectivity and the absence of day-to-day office disruptions, in-flight meetings provide an opportunity for undivided attention. This controlled setting can enhance the efficiency of discussions and contribute to successful deal closures.

Considerations for In-Flight Meetings:

Privacy and Confidentiality:

Private jet travel inherently provides a high level of privacy and confidentiality. This is particularly crucial for discussions involving sensitive information or high-profile clients. The controlled environment of a private jet ensures that conversations remain discreet.

Comfort and Productivity:

Private jets offer a comfortable and conducive environment for work. Seating arrangements can be tailored to facilitate discussions, and amenities on board contribute to a productive atmosphere. Making the most of this comfort can enhance the overall efficiency of the in-flight meeting.

Logistics and Planning:

Effective planning is essential for in-flight meetings. Ensure that the travel schedule aligns with the availability of all parties involved. Coordinate logistics, including ground transportation, to minimize any potential disruptions and maximize the time available for discussions.

Virtual Deals: Mastering Zoom Meetings

Zoom Meetings:

Leverage Technology for Remote Interactions:

Embracing technology is at the core of successful virtual deals. Zoom meetings offer a platform for face-to-face interactions, enabling discussions and negotiations to take place seamlessly, regardless of geographical distances. Leverage the features of Zoom to create an immersive and engaging virtual environment.

Guide Customers Through Online Processes:

In virtual deal-making, it's essential to guide customers through online processes smoothly. This may include walking them through payment setups, document sharing, or any other digital processes relevant to the deal. Providing clear instructions and support during these processes contributes to a positive and efficient virtual experience.

Ensure a Professional Virtual Background:

The visual aspect of a Zoom meeting is crucial. Ensure a professional virtual background to maintain a polished and business-appropriate appearance. This not only enhances your personal brand but also contributes to a distraction-free environment, allowing participants to focus on the content of the discussion.

Minimize Disruptions:

Virtual meetings come with their own set of challenges, including potential disruptions. Minimize background noise, interruptions, and technical glitches to create a smooth and professional meeting experience. Encourage participants to mute their microphones when not speaking and address any technical issues promptly to maintain the flow of the discussion.

Considerations for Zoom Meetings:

Familiarity with Zoom Features:

A thorough understanding of Zoom features is crucial for effective virtual deal-making. Familiarize yourself with functions such as screen sharing, breakout rooms, and chat options to enhance the interactivity of the meeting.

Engagement Strategies:

Virtual meetings can sometimes lack the spontaneity of in-person interactions. Implement engagement strategies, such as interactive presentations, polls, or Q&A sessions, to keep participants actively involved and maintain their interest throughout the meeting.

Testing and Preparation:

Before the scheduled meeting, conduct testing to ensure that your audio, video, and screen-sharing capabilities are functioning correctly. This preparation helps to minimize disruptions during the actual meeting and showcases a level of professionalism to participants.

Mastering the Art of Handling the Price Objection

Addressing the question, "How much is it?" is a pivotal moment in any sales conversation. Your response can shape the prospect's perception of value and influence their decision-making process. Instead of providing a straightforward price, consider employing a strategic and value-driven approach. Here are several effective ways to respond:

1. Highlighting Value:

"I'm glad you're interested! Before we discuss the price, let me share the incredible value you'll receive with our [product/service]. It's not just about the cost; it's about the benefits and solutions it brings to you."

Explanation: By emphasizing value first, you shift the focus from the price tag to the advantages and solutions your offering provides.

2. Qualification and Customization:

"Certainly! The cost can vary based on your specific needs and preferences. To provide you with the most accurate quote, could you share a bit more about [specific requirements]?"

Explanation: This approach encourages further conversation, allowing you to tailor the offering to the prospect's unique needs and potentially justify a higher price.

3. Bundle Offerings:

"I can certainly provide you with the pricing details. Additionally, we have some exclusive bundles that include [additional features or services]. It might be worthwhile to explore those options for a more comprehensive solution."

Explanation: Introducing bundled offerings can create the perception of added value and make the prospect consider a more inclusive package.

4. Comparative Pricing:

"The pricing depends on the features you're looking for. We offer different packages tailored to various needs. In comparison to [competitor], our pricing is competitive, and we provide [unique benefits]."

Explanation: By mentioning a competitor, you position your offering in the context of value and competitiveness, potentially justifying a higher price.

5. ROI Discussion:

"I'd be happy to discuss the pricing with you. Before we delve into that, let's talk about the return on investment. Our [product/service] is designed to deliver [specific outcomes], which can greatly contribute to your [business goals]."

Explanation: Shifting the conversation to the return on investment emphasizes the long-term value and impact of your offering.

6. Payment Options:

"Our pricing is flexible, and we offer various payment options to suit different budgets. Before we discuss the numbers, could you share if you have any specific preferences or requirements?"

Explanation: Discussing payment options can make the prospect feel more in control of the financial aspect and potentially open up discussions about a higher-priced option.

7. Uncover Budget Constraints:

"Certainly, I want to ensure we find the best solution within your budget. Could you give me an idea of the budget range you have in mind? This will help me tailor our offerings to fit your financial preferences."

Explanation: By understanding the prospect's budget constraints, you can align your pricing discussions with their financial comfort zone.

8. Provide a Range:

"Our pricing typically ranges from [lower limit] to [higher limit], depending on the specific features and customization you require. To offer a more accurate quote, could you share your preferences?"

Explanation: Offering a range sets expectations and allows for a more tailored discussion based on the prospect's needs.

One of the most critical moments in a sales conversation is when the client pops the question, "How much does it cost?" Your response at this juncture can either maintain your control or relinquish it entirely. Understanding the psychology behind this question and responding strategically is the key to successful high-ticket closing.

Remember, the key is to steer the conversation toward value, customization, and the prospect's specific needs before delving into the specifics of pricing. This approach positions your offering as a solution rather than just a cost, making it more likely to resonate with the prospect.

The Early Inquiry:

When the client asks about the price early in the conversation, it signifies a desire to cut to the chase, seeking the bottom line without delving into the details. Responding with the exact price at this stage hands over control prematurely.

The "It Depends" Tactic:

Instead of divulging the price right away, respond with "It depends." This invites them to share more about their needs and requirements. Redirect the conversation to understand why they are considering your product or service in the first place.

Guiding the Conversation:

Through this redirection, keep the focus on building a case for your offer. Encourage them to articulate their needs, allowing you to tailor your pitch and create a more compelling case for your product or service.

Mid-Conversation Inquiry:

If the question arises midway through the conversation, and they persist, consider offering a range rather than a fixed price. For example, "It can range from $500 to $1,000, depending on your specific needs. How does that sound to you?"

Continued Engagement:

After providing a price, don't stop there. Continue engaging them with follow-up questions. For instance, ask if the amount is within their budget or if they are comfortable with the proposed expenditure. This opens up further discussion and helps gauge their readiness.

Handling Resistance:

If the client expresses resistance or finds the price unfavorable, be prepared to address their concerns. This might involve justifying the value, emphasizing unique selling points, or revisiting the benefits tailored to their needs.

The Power Dynamic:

In high-ticket closing, it's essential to recognize that as the closer, you hold the power. You dictate when to reveal the price based on the progression of the conversation. This strategic approach ensures you maintain control and lead the client effectively to a successful close.

Understanding Industry Norms:

Different industries have varying practices regarding price disclosure. In some, providing upfront prices is standard, while in others, it's considered premature or even rude. Familiarize yourself with the norms in your industry to ensure you align with expectations.

CHAPTER SIX

Mastering Referral Strategies for Explosive Growth

In the intricate dance of professional relationships, the choice of language can wield unparalleled influence. Whether you're navigating the nuanced world of referrals or forging connections in the business arena, the words you choose can significantly impact the outcome. One such linguistic nuance lies in the substitution of "refer" with "introduce" — a seemingly subtle shift that holds the potential to reshape the dynamics of interaction.

The term "refer" inherently carries a sense of futurity, suggesting a potential action to be taken at some point down the line. This linguistic choice introduces a subtle disconnect, creating a mental gap between the present moment and the envisioned referral. On the other hand, opting for the word "introduce" injects immediacy and a sense of currency into the conversation.

Consider the following scenario: you find yourself inquiring of a colleague or client, "Do you know anyone you could refer to me?" This formulation inadvertently allows for a certain degree of procrastination, as it places the referral action in the realm of the future. The onus is shifted to a later time, and the urgency may dissipate.

Contrastingly, imagine employing the term "introduce" in the same inquiry: "Do you know anyone you could introduce to me?" This subtle change injects a sense of urgency into the conversation, transforming the request into a more immediate call to action. The use of the present tense emphasizes the here and now, prompting a quicker response and potentially expediting the referral process.

Language, in this context, transcends its conventional role as a mere tool of communication. It emerges as a strategic asset, a subtle yet powerful instrument that can shape the course of professional interactions. The switch from "refer" to "introduce" exemplifies the strategic leverage embedded in language, illustrating how a nuanced choice of words can be a catalyst for more prompt and effective results.

Consider the practical application of this linguistic strategy in a real-world scenario. Picture yourself addressing a client with the question, "Do you know anyone who could introduce me to people needing our services?" The utilization of "introduce" in this context not only seeks a recommendation but actively invites immediate engagement. The question becomes a catalyst for action, propelling the conversation forward with a sense of urgency.

Seek Permission Early: A Pledge to Proactive Referrals

In the intricate dance of professional relationships, the art of referrals often takes center stage. However, rather than relegating the discussion of referrals to the periphery, savvy professionals recognize the power of integrating this conversation early on. The strategic move is to seek permission at the inception of a business relationship, setting the stage for proactive engagement and weaving referrals seamlessly into the fabric of the transaction.

Waiting until the end of a transaction to broach the topic of referrals can be akin to closing the stable door after the horse has bolted. To harness the full potential of proactive referrals, it is imperative to lay the groundwork from the outset. This approach not only positions referrals as a natural extension of the business relationship but also ensures that the idea of referrals is not an afterthought but an integral component of the entire client engagement process.

The first step in this strategic maneuver is to ask for permission with a clear and carefully crafted script. By expressing a genuine desire for your clients to become active contributors to your network, you not only demonstrate transparency but also underscore the collaborative nature of your professional journey. The goal is to make referrals an explicit part of the client relationship, fostering a sense of shared purpose and mutual benefit.

Consider the following example script as a template for initiating this crucial conversation:

"Before we even embark on our journey together, may I seek your commitment to introducing me to at least two people you care about by the end of our transaction?"

This script serves as a strategic invitation, seamlessly integrating the concept of referrals into the early stages of the professional relationship. By framing the request as a commitment and expressing a specific numerical goal, you not only demonstrate the importance of referrals to your business but also provide a clear and tangible expectation for your client.

The proactive approach to referrals, initiated through early permission-seeking, transforms the dynamic of the client relationship. It establishes a shared understanding that referrals are not only welcome but actively encouraged. This upfront commitment not only increases the likelihood of subsequent referrals but also reinforces the collaborative nature of the business alliance.

In the realm of cultivating professional relationships, particularly with high-net-worth individuals, the ability to navigate subtle nuances becomes paramount. While the direct ask for referrals may at times evoke unease, a strategic pivot to seeking advice can be a nuanced approach that opens doors to invaluable opportunities. Positioning yourself as someone seeking the wisdom of your clients not only allows you to glean insights but also creates a natural pathway for them to organically recommend your services to their network.

Understanding the intricacies of your clients is a fundamental aspect of this approach. High-net-worth individuals, in particular, may be sensitive to direct solicitations for referrals. Hence, the art lies in reframing the conversation, positioning yourself as a seeker of advice rather than a solicitor of referrals. This shift in approach transforms the dynamic from transactional to relational, fostering a deeper connection with your clients.

Consider employing the following example approach:

"I truly value your perspective. In your experience, how would you suggest I encourage others to connect with me when they are in need of our services?"

This framing not only acknowledges the client's expertise but also presents the request as an opportunity for them to share their valuable insights. By seeking advice, you tap into their knowledge while subtly creating a pathway for them to recommend your services based on their own wisdom.

However, in the intricate dance of referrals, not every request is met with an immediate affirmation. Rejections or hesitations, far from being roadblocks, are actually opportunities to refine your approach. The key lies in transforming these moments into constructive dialogues that deepen the understanding of your client's reservations.

When faced with a "no" or an "I can't think of anyone," don't view it as a closed door. Instead, embrace it as an opening to further explore their perspective. Shift the conversation by asking a follow-up question:

"I understand. What would need to happen for you to feel comfortable introducing me to others who might benefit from our services? Your insights are crucial in shaping our approach."

This response not only demonstrates your commitment to respecting their boundaries but also provides valuable insights into any hesitations they might have. It transforms a potential obstacle into an opportunity for collaboration, reinforcing the relational aspect of the client relationship.

As you embark on the journey of mastering referral strategies, remember that these techniques are not static principles; they are dynamic tools meant to be applied with finesse and adapted to the unique dynamics of each client relationship. Referrals should not be left to chance; they should be an intentional and integrated part of your sales arsenal.

CHAPTER SEVEN

Decoding the "Send Me a Quote" Objection

In the intricate dance of sales, the phrase "send me a quote" is a familiar refrain, echoing through countless B2B and B2C interactions. The prospect, seemingly interested, throws out this request as a bridge between conversation and commitment. However, as any seasoned sales professional knows, this isn't always a genuine expression of intent. In this chapter, we dissect this common objection and unveil three potent ways to cut through the smoke and mirrors, getting to the heart of the prospect's true intentions.

The Power of Agreement and Clarification

In the intricate dance of sales, the way you respond to certain requests can be the linchpin that determines the trajectory of the entire interaction. When confronted with the seemingly straightforward yet pivotal "send me a quote" request, the initial response becomes a crucial moment in the sales process. Instead of instinctively resisting or merely complying, savvy sales professionals recognize the power of embracing the prospect's request with enthusiasm while simultaneously seeking immediate clarification.

The approach begins with a strategic pivot: "I'll be more than happy to. Based on what we've discussed so far, does this sound like something you would go with?"

This response is more than a mere acknowledgment of the prospect's request; it is a nuanced maneuver that intertwines agreement with the art of clarification. By expressing genuine enthusiasm, you align yourself with the prospect's needs, signaling a willingness to meet their expectations. Simultaneously, the follow-up question seeks to crystallize the prospect's level of interest and commitment.

The power lies in the duality of this response. On one hand, you are saying, "Yes, I am ready to provide you with the information you seek," demonstrating your responsiveness and eagerness to move the conversation forward. On the other hand, the question subtly probes the prospect's intent, prompting them to clarify their stance on moving forward with the discussed proposal.

Consider the potential outcomes of this nuanced approach:

Immediate Agreement: If the prospect responds positively, expressing agreement with your proposed solution, you have successfully aligned yourself with their needs and obtained a preliminary buy-in. This sets the stage for a more focused and tailored quotation process.

Clarification Request: In cases where the prospect hesitates or seeks further clarification, you open a constructive dialogue to address any concerns or uncertainties. This not only allows you to refine your understanding of their needs but also positions you as a consultative partner, committed to ensuring the proposed solution aligns with their objectives.

Reassessment Opportunity: If the response indicates a misalignment between the discussed solution and the prospect's expectations, it provides an opportunity to revisit and refine your proposal before proceeding with the quotation. This preemptive reassessment demonstrates flexibility and a genuine commitment to delivering value.

In the dynamic landscape of sales, the power of agreement and clarification serves as a strategic tool to navigate the nuanced terrain of prospect interactions. By seamlessly combining affirmation with a clarifying question, sales professionals can cut through ambiguity, align with prospect expectations, and pave the way for more targeted and effective sales processes.

The Comparative Inquiry: Unveiling the Competition

In the intricate landscape of sales, understanding the nuances of a prospect's decision-making process is a critical skill that sets top-notch professionals apart. When faced with the request for a quote, the strategic deployment of a comparative inquiry can unveil valuable insights into the prospect's considerations, shedding light on their priorities and preferences.

The approach begins with an affirmative response to the prospect's request: "I'll be more than happy to send you some quotes in writing." This signals your commitment to providing the information they seek while maintaining a positive and cooperative tone. However, the true power lies in the follow-up question that deftly leverages the dynamics of comparison: "How does this compare to other quotes you've received so far?"

This comparative inquiry serves as a subtle yet potent tool to encourage transparency about the prospect's decision-making landscape. By explicitly inviting them to share insights on how your offering stacks up against others, you open a dialogue that goes beyond mere price considerations. This approach unveils whether their primary focus is on cost or if they are seeking additional value in the proposed solution.

Consider the potential outcomes of this strategic maneuver:

Price Sensitivity: If the prospect emphasizes price as a significant factor in their decision-making, this insight allows you to tailor your approach accordingly. It may prompt a discussion on the unique value proposition your solution offers or the potential for customized packages that align with their budgetary constraints.

Value-Oriented Considerations: If the prospect highlights elements beyond price, such as the features, benefits, or additional services offered, it provides a nuanced understanding of their priorities. This knowledge enables you to emphasize the distinctive value your solution brings to the table, steering the conversation toward the aspects that resonate most with the prospect.

Competitor Insights: By learning about the other quotes in consideration, you gain valuable intelligence about the competitive landscape. This knowledge empowers you to position your offering strategically, addressing potential gaps or differentiating factors that may influence the prospect's decision.

In the dynamic realm of sales, the comparative inquiry serves as a multifaceted tool, transcending the transactional nature of a quote request. It transforms the interaction into a collaborative exploration of fit and value, allowing you to adapt your approach based on the prospect's unique considerations.

Budget Alignment: Direct and Decisive

In the intricate realm of sales, the prospect's request for a written quote often serves as a subtle inquiry into the alignment of the proposed solution with their budgetary considerations. Recognizing and addressing this underlying question directly can be a pivotal moment in steering the conversation toward a more decisive axis. When faced with the request for a quote, a direct and unequivocal response that tackles the issue of budget compatibility head-on can foster transparency and set the stage for a more focused discussion.

The strategic approach involves responding with clarity and assurance: "Absolutely, I'll be more than happy to. Based on the quote or the price I've given you so far, does this sound like it fits within your budget?"

This direct inquiry cuts through ambiguity, positioning the conversation on a decisive axis. By explicitly addressing the prospect's budgetary considerations, you create an opportunity for an open and honest dialogue about financial parameters. This approach not only demonstrates your commitment to understanding the prospect's needs but also allows you to proactively address any potential concerns related to budget constraints.

Consider the potential outcomes of this direct and decisive approach:

Affirmative Response: If the prospect confirms that the proposed quote aligns with their budget, it signals a positive step toward potential alignment and agreement. This affirmation provides a foundation for moving forward with confidence, knowing that the financial parameters are in sync with the prospect's expectations.

Budgetary Discussion: In cases where the prospect expresses reservations or hesitations regarding the proposed quote, the direct inquiry opens the door for a constructive discussion about budget considerations. This dialogue allows you to explore potential adjustments or modifications to better meet the prospect's financial constraints while maintaining the value of the proposed solution.

Bonus: The Future-oriented Scenario Analysis

To uncover deeper insights and position the conversation within a future-oriented context, consider incorporating a scenario analysis into your interaction. Present a hypothetical scenario with the question: "Let's pretend I send you the quote and the proposal, and you like what you see. What's going to happen next?"

This scenario analysis not only provides clarity on the prospect's timeline for decision-making but also offers insights into their readiness to proceed. Whether the response indicates an immediate commitment or a consideration for the future, this question allows you to tailor your follow-up strategy accordingly. It provides a glimpse into the prospect's decision-making process and aids in aligning your actions with their expectations.

CHAPTER EIGHT

The Art of Stopping and Listening in Sales

The Echo of Concerns: Reading Back the Customer's Narrative

One of the most impactful gestures a salesperson can make is to articulate the customer's concerns in their own words. When a customer expresses their needs, challenges, or aspirations, the attentive salesperson not only hears the words but absorbs the essence of their narrative. Repeating these concerns back to the customer demonstrates a profound level of engagement and signals that their voice has been not just heard but truly understood.

Building Trust Through Reflection:

Validation of Customer's Importance: By echoing the customer's concerns, the salesperson communicates that the customer's perspective is not only acknowledged but valued.

Demonstration of Active Listening: The act of summarizing and reflecting points back to the customer reinforces that the salesperson is actively engaged in the conversation, not merely waiting for their turn to speak.

2. Bridging the Gap: Understanding Beyond Words

Listening goes beyond the spoken word; it involves decoding the nuances, the unspoken cues that reveal the customer's true sentiments. As the salesperson listens attentively, they become attuned to the customer's emotions, hesitations, and underlying motivations. This empathetic connection bridges the gap between a transactional exchange and a genuine, trust-based relationship.

Non-Verbal Cues:

Body Language and Facial Expressions: A perceptive salesperson pays attention to the customer's body language and facial expressions, gauging reactions that may go unspoken.

Tone and Inflection: Variations in tone and inflection can convey excitement, frustration, or uncertainty. A keen ear captures these subtleties, allowing the salesperson to respond with heightened sensitivity.

3. Trust as the Foundation: Nurturing Authentic Connections

Trust is the bedrock upon which enduring relationships are built. The simple act of listening, understanding, and reflecting back the customer's concerns fosters an environment of trust. This trust extends beyond the transaction at hand, laying the groundwork for future interactions and customer loyalty.

Customer-Centric Approach:

Putting the Customer First: By actively listening, the salesperson communicates a commitment to prioritizing the customer's needs over the immediate goal of making a sale.

Responsive Problem Solving: Understanding the customer's concerns allows the salesperson to tailor solutions that directly address their unique challenges, showcasing a genuine interest in solving problems.

4. The Impact on Decision-Making: Empowering Customer Choices

Listening empowers customers by making them feel seen, heard, and respected. This empowerment is a catalyst for informed decision-making. When a salesperson recaps the customer's concerns, they provide a roadmap for collaborative decision-making, ensuring that the final choice aligns seamlessly with the customer's priorities.

Informed Decision-Making:

Clarity in Options: By summarizing the customer's concerns, the salesperson ensures that the available options are presented with clarity, making it easier for the customer to make decisions.

Alignment with Customer Motivations: The choices presented resonate with the customer's motivations and priorities, leading to decisions that are not just logical but emotionally satisfying.

5. The Continuum of Trust: From Transaction to Relationship

The art of listening transforms a one-time transaction into the beginning of a relationship. As the salesperson invests time and attention in understanding the customer's narrative, trust becomes a continuous thread woven through every interaction. This continuum of trust lays the groundwork for enduring partnerships, customer loyalty, and positive word-of-mouth referrals.

Long-Term Relationship Building:

Consistent Engagement: The salesperson's commitment to attentive listening remains consistent over time, reinforcing the trust established in the initial stages.

Anticipation of Evolving Needs: Through ongoing listening, the salesperson stays attuned to the customer's evolving needs, positioning themselves as a reliable partner in the customer's journey.

The Temptation to Interrupt: Understanding the Urge

In the fast-paced world of sales, the temptation to interrupt can be significant. Sales professionals, eager to demonstrate their expertise or accelerate the conversation, may find themselves on the verge of interjecting before the customer has fully expressed their concerns or motivations. However, yielding to this impulse can have unintended consequences.

Understanding the Urge to Interrupt:

Desire to Showcase Expertise: Sales professionals often interrupt with the intention of showcasing their knowledge and offering prompt solutions.

Time-Pressure Dilemma: The pressure to meet targets and close deals within limited time frames can heighten the temptation to expedite the conversation.

2. The Impact of Patience: Allowing the Customer to Unfold

Exercising patience in the sales process involves letting the customer unfold their thoughts, needs, and concerns without premature interference. This patience creates a space for the customer to feel heard, valued, and understood.

Benefits of Patient Listening:

Building Trust: Patient listening fosters trust as customers feel that their concerns are given the time and attention they deserve.

Understanding Nuances: Allowing the customer to unfold reveals nuances that might be missed in a hurried exchange, contributing to a more comprehensive understanding of their needs.

3. The Dangers of Prejudgment: Narrowing Possibilities

Prejudging customer needs is akin to closing a door before fully exploring the possibilities behind it. When a sales professional makes assumptions about what the customer needs or can afford, they risk limiting the scope of the conversation and potentially missing out on valuable opportunities.

Dangers of Prejudgment:

Narrowing Sales Opportunities: Prejudging may result in steering the conversation towards what the salesperson assumes the customer needs, potentially overlooking more lucrative opportunities.

Undermining Customer Trust: Customers can sense when they are being pigeonholed, and this can undermine trust and rapport.

4. Embracing Open-Ended Inquiry: Inviting Complete Narratives

To counteract the urge to prejudge, sales professionals can adopt the practice of open-ended inquiry. This involves asking questions that encourage customers to share more about their needs, motivations, and challenges.

Open-Ended Inquiry Techniques:

"What brings you here today?"

"Could you tell me more about your goals or concerns?"

"How can our product/service best meet your requirements?"

5. Uncovering Hidden Opportunities: Beyond Initial Assumptions

Patient listening opens the door to uncovering hidden opportunities. When customers feel free to express themselves fully, the sales professional gains insights that may lead to additional sales, upselling, or a more strategic alignment with the customer's goals.

Uncovering Hidden Opportunities:

Identifying Upselling Potential: Patient listening allows the sales professional to identify areas where additional products or services could enhance the customer's experience.

Strategic Alignment: Understanding the customer's long-term goals enables the salesperson to position their offerings as integral components of the customer's strategic plans.

6. Transforming Challenges into Solutions: Guided by Customer Insights

By resisting the urge to prejudge and patiently listening to the customer's complete narrative, sales professionals can transform challenges into innovative solutions. This customer-centric approach ensures that the proposed solutions are aligned with the customer's actual needs, enhancing the likelihood of a successful transaction.

Guided by Customer Insights:

Tailoring Solutions: Insights gained through patient listening empower the sales professional to tailor solutions that precisely address the customer's unique challenges.

Enhancing Customer Satisfaction: A solution crafted based on comprehensive understanding not only meets but exceeds customer expectations, fostering satisfaction and loyalty.

CHAPTER NINE

The Art of Customer Response Analysis

In the intricate dance of sales, the ability to keenly observe and interpret customer responses is a skill that elevates a sales professional from good to exceptional. Every nuance, from body language to verbal cues, provides valuable insights into the prospect's mindset and receptiveness. In this chapter, we delve into the art of customer response analysis, exploring key indicators and strategies to adapt based on these observations.

Reading Body Language: Decoding the Unspoken:

Posture:

Leaning Forward:

A prospect's posture can reveal a great deal about their level of interest and engagement. Leaning forward is often a positive indicator, suggesting that the prospect is attentive and interested in the conversation. It signals openness and a willingness to actively participate in the interaction.

Crossed Arms:

Conversely, crossed arms can convey defensiveness or a guarded attitude. This posture may indicate that the prospect is not fully receptive or may have reservations. Acknowledging and addressing these concerns in a tactful manner can help in building trust and breaking down barriers.

Comfort Level:

Observing overall body posture, such as whether the prospect appears relaxed or tense, provides insights into their comfort level. A relaxed posture may indicate a sense of ease, while tension could suggest discomfort or unease. Adjusting your approach based on these cues can contribute to creating a more comfortable and positive environment.

Blinking:

Rapid Blinking:

The rate of blinking can offer additional cues about a prospect's emotional state. Rapid blinking may indicate stress, nervousness, or discomfort. In such cases, it's important to approach the conversation with sensitivity, perhaps slowing down the pace or addressing any concerns to alleviate tension.

Slower Blinking:

Conversely, slower blinking can signal focus and concentration. When a prospect is deeply engaged in the conversation or processing information, their blinking rate may slow down. Recognizing this can affirm that the prospect is absorbing the content and may be receptive to more detailed information or a deeper discussion.

Adjusting Your Approach:

Ease Tension:

If body language suggests tension or discomfort, consider adjusting your approach to ease the prospect's concerns. This might involve addressing any objections, clarifying information, or simply adopting a more relaxed conversational tone.

Tailor Your Message:

Adapting your message based on body language cues is crucial for maintaining engagement. If the prospect leans forward with interest, you may choose to delve into more detailed aspects of your offering. On the other hand, if signs of defensiveness are present, focusing on building rapport and addressing concerns may take precedence.

Deciphering Verbal Responses: Unveiling Intentions

Tone and Content:

Tone:

Enthusiasm:

The tone of a prospect's voice can be a powerful indicator of their level of enthusiasm. A vibrant and positive tone often suggests genuine interest and excitement. Recognizing this enthusiasm allows sales professionals to build on the prospect's positive energy and tailor their communication to further amplify the excitement.

Skepticism:

Conversely, a skeptical or cautious tone may be reflected through a more measured and reserved delivery. Recognizing tones of skepticism enables sales professionals to address concerns proactively, providing additional information or reassurances to build trust and alleviate reservations.

Uncertainty:

A tone tinged with uncertainty may indicate that the prospect is still weighing options or is not fully convinced. This provides an opportunity for sales professionals to offer clarifications, additional details, or personalized insights that can help the prospect make a more informed decision.

Content:

Priorities and Concerns:

Analyzing the content of verbal responses uncovers valuable insights into a prospect's priorities and concerns. If a prospect expresses excitement about specific features or benefits, it indicates elements that resonate with them. Sales professionals can then strategically emphasize these aspects in their pitch to align with the prospect's preferences.

Reservations:

Conversely, if a prospect voices reservations or raises specific concerns, it is crucial to address these directly. Acknowledging and addressing objections demonstrates attentiveness and a willingness to engage in a transparent and solution-oriented conversation. It also allows sales professionals to tailor their pitch to alleviate concerns and build confidence.

Adjusting Your Approach:

Amplify Excitement:

When the prospect's tone indicates enthusiasm, seize the opportunity to amplify that excitement. Highlight key features or benefits that align with their expressed interests, creating a more personalized and engaging pitch.

Address Concerns:

In the face of reservations or concerns, adjust your approach to address these head-on. Provide additional information, share success stories, or offer assurances that directly speak to the prospect's apprehensions. This tailored response demonstrates a commitment to understanding and resolving their specific concerns.

Analyzing Breathing Patterns: Gauging Emotional States
Rhythm and Depth:

Rhythm and Depth:

Shallow or Irregular Breathing:

Observing a prospect's breathing patterns is akin to tapping into their emotional responses. Shallow or irregular breathing may signify stress, discomfort, or unease. These patterns may emerge in response to challenging questions, objections, or moments of uncertainty. Recognizing these signs allows sales professionals to respond with empathy and navigate the conversation with sensitivity.

Steady, Deep Breaths:

Conversely, steady and deep breaths suggest a sense of calmness and composure. When a prospect's breathing is measured and controlled, it often indicates a more relaxed and receptive state. Sales professionals can interpret this as a positive sign, signaling that the prospect is open to the discussion and engaged in the conversation.

Using Breathing Patterns to Gauge Emotional States:

Adjusting Your Pace:

In moments of stress or discomfort indicated by shallow or irregular breathing, sales professionals can adjust their pace. Slowing down the conversation and allowing for pauses can provide the prospect with the mental space to process information and ease tension. A deliberate and measured approach can be calming in these situations.

Adapting Your Tone:

Understanding a prospect's emotional state through breathing patterns enables sales professionals to adapt their tone accordingly. In situations where reassurance is needed, a soothing and empathetic tone can help build trust. Conversely, in moments of enthusiasm or receptiveness, maintaining an upbeat and engaging tone can capitalize on positive emotions.

Offering Support:

If shallow or irregular breathing persists, it may be an indication that the prospect needs additional support or clarification. Sales professionals can proactively offer assistance, address concerns, and provide information to alleviate stress. This approach demonstrates a commitment to understanding and meeting the prospect's needs.

Considerations for Reading Breathing Patterns:

Context Awareness:

Interpreting breathing patterns requires context awareness. Consider the overall flow of the conversation, the topics being discussed, and the prospect's body language to gain a comprehensive understanding of their emotional state.

Non-Intrusive Observation:

Observing breathing patterns should be done non-intrusively. Maintain a focus on the conversation while subtly noting changes in the prospect's breathing. Avoid drawing attention to this observation, as it may disrupt the natural flow of the interaction.

Question Dynamics: Assessing Engagement and Curiosity
Frequency and Type:

Frequency and Type:

Engaged Questions:

An engaged buyer is often characterized by the quality and frequency of their questions. They seek to delve into specific details about product features, benefits, and potential outcomes. These questions demonstrate a genuine interest in understanding the nuances of the offering and signal a proactive approach to decision-making.

Disinterest or Minimal Queries:

Conversely, disinterest or a lack of engagement may manifest in minimal or generic queries. A prospect who is less invested in the conversation may ask fewer questions or pose inquiries that lack depth. Recognizing these cues is crucial for sales professionals to adapt their approach and re-ignite interest.

Tailoring Your Responses:

Specific Queries:

When faced with specific and detailed questions, sales professionals should respond in kind. Provide in-depth information, address nuances, and showcase a comprehensive understanding of the prospect's concerns. This approach aligns with the prospect's engagement level and reinforces the value of the offering.

Broad Queries:

In scenarios where questions are broad or generic, sales professionals should offer overarching benefits and key highlights. Tailor responses to provide a high-level overview that captures the prospect's attention and conveys the broader value proposition. This adaptability showcases attentiveness to the prospect's needs and preferences.

Adaptability in Question Response:

Showcase Attentiveness:

Adapting responses based on the type of questions reflects a sales professional's attentiveness to the prospect's communication style and level of interest. This responsiveness builds rapport and fosters a sense of partnership in the decision-making process.

Demonstrate Value:

Tailoring responses not only meets the prospect where they are in their buying journey but also allows sales professionals to strategically emphasize the value proposition. Whether diving into specifics or providing a broad overview, each response should reinforce the unique benefits and advantages of the offering.

Considerations for Question Dynamics:

Contextual Awareness:

Assessing question dynamics requires contextual awareness. Consider the prospect's industry, role, and specific needs to interpret the significance of their questions accurately.

Two-Way Communication:

Question dynamics create a two-way communication flow. Encourage prospects to ask questions by fostering an open and inviting environment. This not only provides valuable insights but also enhances the overall engagement of the interaction.

Evaluating Payment Commitment: Gauging Confidence and Assurance

Realism and Confidence:

Realism and Confidence:

Unwavering Commitment:

A prospect's commitment to payment is often reflected in the unwavering nature of their assurances. If they express a strong commitment and provide a realistic timeline for payment, it indicates a higher degree of certainty and confidence in their decision. This unwavering stance is a positive indicator of their intent to move forward with the deal.

Realistic Timeline:

Assessing the realism of the payment commitment involves evaluating the timeline provided by the prospect. A realistic timeline aligns with industry standards, the complexity of the product or service, and the prospect's internal processes. If the prospect provides a timeline that is feasible and corresponds with these factors, it reinforces their commitment and increases the likelihood of a successful deal.

Identifying Potential Obstacles:

Vague Assurances:

Vague assurances or general statements about payment commitment may indicate a lack of clarity or potential hesitancy. If the prospect is not providing specific details or is hesitant in their commitments, it raises a red flag. Sales professionals should proactively seek clarification and address any underlying concerns or uncertainties.

Hesitancy:

Hesitancy in expressing commitment to payment could be a signal of potential obstacles or objections. Instead of overlooking these signs, sales professionals should probe gently to uncover the root of the hesitation.

Understanding the prospect's concerns allows for a targeted and strategic approach to addressing those issues.

Tailoring Your Approach:

Instilling Confidence:

In the face of vague assurances or hesitancy, sales professionals should focus on instilling confidence in the prospect. This may involve providing additional information, offering assurances, or addressing any lingering doubts. Demonstrating a clear understanding of the prospect's concerns and actively working to resolve them builds trust and confidence in the sales process.

Proactive Assurance:

Proactively addressing potential obstacles is a key element of tailoring the approach to evaluate payment commitment. Anticipate concerns that may arise based on the prospect's industry, company size, or specific needs. Providing proactive assurance can help preemptively alleviate doubts and reinforce the prospect's confidence in moving forward.

Considerations for Payment Commitment:

Contextual Understanding:

Assessing payment commitment requires a deep understanding of the prospect's context. Consider factors such as their industry norms, budget constraints, and decision-making processes to contextualize their payment commitments effectively.

Open Communication:

Foster open communication with the prospect throughout the sales process. Encourage them to express any concerns or hesitations they may have about payment commitments. This transparency creates a collaborative environment and allows for the timely resolution of any issues.

CHAPTER TEN

Crafting Irresistible Offers – The Art of Persuasion

In the intricate dance of business, where transactions are the heartbeat, the art of crafting an offer stands as a pivotal skill. Join me as we unravel the secrets of an irresistible offer, drawing inspiration from the timeless wisdom of the business world.

The Power of Persuasion: An Offer They Can't Refuse

At the heart of triumphant business transactions lies the profound ability to craft an offer that transcends resistance. In my journey through the realms of entrepreneurship, one lesson has resonated louder than most—the power of an offer they can't refuse. It's not solely about the price tag attached; rather, it's about skillfully weaving a tapestry of value that renders the notion of refusal unthinkable.

Understanding the Dynamics of Persuasion

Persuasion is an art that goes beyond mere convincing; it's about creating an irresistible proposition. The dynamics of persuasion involve tapping into the prospect's desires, addressing their pain points, and crafting an offer that aligns seamlessly with their aspirations. It's a delicate dance where the sales professional becomes a master storyteller, narrating a tale where the prospect is the hero and the offer, their ultimate reward.

Beyond Price: Weaving a Tapestry of Value

While price is undoubtedly a factor, the power of persuasion extends far beyond a numerical figure. It involves weaving a tapestry of value that encompasses the unique features, benefits, and solutions offered. The prospect should not just see the cost but should be immersed in a narrative where the investment is a gateway to transformation, efficiency, or enhancement of their current state.

Identifying and Addressing Pain Points

A persuasive offer begins with a profound understanding of the prospect's pain points. What keeps them up at night? What challenges are they grappling with? By identifying these pain points, the sales professional can tailor the offer to serve as a remedy, positioning the product or service as the solution they've been seeking.

Creating a Sense of Urgency

The art of persuasion often involves creating a sense of urgency. Whether through limited-time offers, exclusive deals, or the anticipation of future benefits, instilling a sense of urgency compels the prospect to act. It transforms the offer from a mere consideration into a compelling opportunity that demands immediate attention.

Crafting Personalized Solutions

Persuasion is most potent when the offer feels personalized. Tailoring the proposal to meet the prospect's specific needs and preferences enhances the sense of value. A personalized offer communicates that the sales professional has invested time in understanding the prospect's unique situation, fostering a deeper connection and trust.

Building Trust Through Transparency

Trust is a cornerstone of effective persuasion. Being transparent about what the offer entails, including potential limitations or considerations, builds trust with the prospect. Transparency creates an atmosphere where the prospect feels informed and confident, making them more likely to embrace the offer wholeheartedly.

Anticipating and Addressing Objections

In the pursuit of an offer they can't refuse, anticipating and addressing objections is crucial. The persuasive sales professional not only presents an enticing offer but also preempts potential hesitations. By incorporating objection-handling strategies into the offer, the salesperson reinforces the idea that every concern has been thoughtfully considered.

Closing the Deal with Confidence

The pinnacle of the persuasion journey is the moment of closure. Armed with an offer they can't refuse, objection-handling finesse, and a deep understanding of the prospect's needs, the sales professional confidently guides the prospect towards a positive decision. The closing of the deal is not a mere transaction but the culmination of a persuasive masterpiece.

Price vs. Value: Unraveling the Equation

"Price is only an issue in the absence of value," a timeless truth etched in the annals of commerce. The delicate equilibrium between what is asked and what is offered pivots on the axis of perceived value. The challenge lies in ensuring that when the prospect is faced with the proposition, the notion of saying no becomes unfathomable.

The Fundamental Truth of Pricing

The mantra that "price is only an issue in the absence of value" encapsulates a fundamental truth in the world of commerce. It underscores the notion that the perceived value of a product or service should eclipse any concern about its price. The artistry in sales involves masterfully presenting and elevating the value proposition, making the price a secondary consideration.

Perceived Value: The Key to Overcoming Price Concerns

Perceived value is the linchpin in unraveling the price vs. value equation. It is not just about the features and benefits of the offering but how these elements are framed in the prospect's mind. The sales professional, like a skilled storyteller, crafts a narrative where the value derived from the product or service becomes an indispensable part of the prospect's vision for a better future.

Aligning Features with Customer Needs

A crucial aspect of presenting value is aligning the features of the offering with the specific needs and desires of the customer. It's not a one-size-fits-all approach but a tailored demonstration of how the product or service addresses the unique challenges or aspirations of the prospect. This alignment reinforces the idea that the offering is not just a commodity but a personalized solution.

Creating a Comparative Advantage

To navigate the price vs. value conundrum, the sales professional aims to create a comparative advantage. This involves highlighting aspects of the offering that set it apart from competitors, emphasizing unique strengths, and showcasing how the prospect stands to gain more from choosing this particular product or service. A distinctive comparative advantage tilts the scales in favor of value.

Building a Narrative of Transformation

The value proposition is not merely a list of attributes; it is a narrative of transformation. The sales professional crafts a story where the prospect envisions a positive change in their circumstances through the adoption of the offering. This narrative transcends the immediate cost considerations, painting a vivid picture of the benefits and outcomes awaiting the prospect.

Overcoming Price Resistance with Added Value

Price resistance often emerges when the perceived value is not explicitly communicated. The sales professional, armed with an understanding of the prospect's needs, addresses this resistance by consistently emphasizing the added value that comes with the offering. Whether it's enhanced features, extended support, or exclusive benefits, the goal is to tip the scales towards an undeniable proposition.

The Continuous Cycle of Value Reinforcement

Unraveling the price vs. value equation is not a one-time endeavor but a continuous cycle of value reinforcement. Through every interaction, the sales professional reiterates and enhances the value proposition, solidifying its presence in the prospect's mind. This ongoing process ensures that the prospect remains convinced of the unparalleled value offered.

The Art of Making Saying "Yes" Irresistible

In the delicate dance between price and value, the ultimate aim is to make saying "yes" irresistible. By elevating the perceived value to a point where it eclipses any hesitations about the price, the sales professional creates a proposition that aligns seamlessly with the prospect's goals and aspirations. The prospect, faced with such an offer, finds it inconceivable to utter the word "no."

The Consequence of No: A Unique Proposition

In my world, a rejection of my offer triggers a unique consequence. The prospect knows that a refusal isn't merely declining a deal; it invites a visit from one of my associates, armed with a baseball bat. It's a dramatic twist that underlines the gravity of turning down an offer from Don Corleone.

A Dramatic Turn of Events

In the world of sales, introducing a consequence for saying "no" adds a touch of drama and urgency to the negotiation process. While it may not involve actual baseball bats, the symbolic weight of the consequence emphasizes the gravity of the decision. The prospect is compelled to consider not just the immediate deal but the potential repercussions of rejecting the offer.

The Psychology of Consequences

The introduction of consequences taps into the psychology of decision-making. It creates a scenario where the prospect must weigh the risks and benefits not only of the offer itself but also of the potential aftermath. This heightened sense of consequence adds an emotional layer to the decision, influencing the prospect's perception and increasing the stakes of their choice.

Leveraging Symbolism

While the consequence may be symbolic, its impact is real in the mind of the prospect. The baseball bat becomes a symbol of missed opportunities, and the prospect envisions the potential outcomes of not seizing the presented offer. Symbolism is a powerful tool that engages the prospect's imagination and emotions, making the decision more profound and thought-provoking.

An Unconventional Approach to Closing

The consequence of "no" introduces an unconventional approach to closing deals. It disrupts the traditional notion of a simple acceptance or rejection and introduces an element of intrigue and consequence. This approach is not just about making a sale; it's about creating a memorable and impactful experience for the prospect, ensuring that the decision-making process is anything but ordinary.

Balancing Drama and Professionalism

While the introduction of consequences adds drama, it's crucial to balance this with professionalism. The goal is not to intimidate but to create a sense of urgency and importance around the decision. The prospect should feel the weight of their choice without feeling coerced or pressured. Striking this balance ensures that the approach is effective in conveying the gravity of the decision.

The Dichotomy of Price vs. Value: A Consumer's Mental Scale

Understanding the psychology of consumer decision-making is crucial. The perpetual battle between price and value rages in the consumer's mind. The key is not just to present an offer but to ensure that the value surpasses the price tag. This, in essence, is the heartbeat of an irresistible proposition.

Elevating Value to Tip the Scale

In the dichotomy of price vs. value, the sales professional's task is to elevate the perceived value to a point where it tips the mental scale in favor of the offer. The consequence of saying "no" serves as a reminder of what is at stake and encourages the prospect to reevaluate the value they stand to gain by accepting the offer. It becomes a psychological nudge that tilts the scales towards acceptance.

Crafting an Irresistible Proposition

An irresistible proposition goes beyond the traditional elements of an offer. It involves creating an experience, an emotional connection, and a sense of consequence. By integrating the consequence of "no" into the sales process, the proposition becomes unique, memorable, and difficult for the prospect to dismiss lightly.

Seven Traits of Irresistible Offers: A Blueprint for Success

In the intricate world of sales, crafting an irresistible offer is an art form that requires finesse and strategic thinking. A blueprint for success emerges from understanding and integrating seven key traits into your offers.

1. Easy to Understand: Clarity is Key

An irresistible offer is one that doesn't leave the prospect puzzled. It revolves around a single, easy-to-understand idea. Complexity becomes a barrier; simplicity, the guiding light. Clear communication ensures that the prospect grasps the value proposition effortlessly, paving the way for a swift and confident decision.

2. Highly Desirable: Tapping into Wants, Not Just Needs

People don't buy solely based on needs; they buy what they want. An irresistible offer taps into the desires of the prospect, whether it's to escape pain or embrace pleasure. Understanding and aligning with these desires elevate the offer from a practical solution to an emotionally compelling proposition.

3. High Perceived Value: What's Valuable to the Consumer

Value alone is not enough; it must be perceived as high value by the consumer. It's not about what you think; it's about what they believe. The sales professional's task is to highlight and emphasize the aspects of the offer that the prospect finds most valuable, creating a perception of a deal too good to pass up.

4. Easy to Get: Simplifying the Path to Yes

No matter how attractive an offer may be, it loses its charm if the path to acquiring it is convoluted. Simplicity in the buying process is a trait of irresistible offers. Whether it's a straightforward checkout process, minimal paperwork, or a user-friendly interface, removing barriers to acceptance enhances the appeal of the offer.

5. Believable and Credible: The Trust Factor

Skepticism often arises when an offer sounds too good to be true. Building trust involves explaining the rationale behind the compelling offer, making it believable and credible. Providing evidence, testimonials, or transparent information reinforces the authenticity of the offer and instills confidence in the prospect.

6. Low Risk or No Risk: Eliminating Hesitation

Consumers fear making the wrong decision. An irresistible offer addresses this fear by reducing or eliminating risk. Money-back guarantees, trial periods, or hassle-free returns create a safety net for the prospect, alleviating hesitations and encouraging them to take the plunge.

7. Urgency: The Catalyst for Action

Procrastination is the enemy of sales. Urgency provides the necessary push for action. Limited-time offers, quantity restrictions, or exclusive bonuses create a sense of immediacy. By introducing a time-sensitive element, the offer becomes more compelling, prompting the prospect to act promptly.

Testimonials of Transformation: A Symphony of Success

The impact of irresistible offers is not theoretical; it's tangible. Through testimonials and success stories, we witness lives transformed, businesses flourishing, and revenues soaring. The force of persuasion, embedded in these offers, has left an indelible mark on those who embraced its principles. These testimonials serve as a symphony of success, echoing the transformative power of irresistible offers.

CHAPTER ELEVEN

The Seven Dumb Questions in Sales: A Cautionary Tale

In the dynamic arena of sales, where every word wields the power to tip the scales between success and failure, the questions you ask are a strategic compass guiding the trajectory of your interactions. In this chapter, we embark on a journey to dissect the cringe-worthy world of dumb questions in sales and unveil the art of crafting inquiries that propel conversations forward.

The Perils of Dumb Questions

Dumb questions, often born out of haste or lack of preparation, can derail a sales conversation before it gains momentum. They signal a lack of understanding, diminish credibility, and leave the prospect questioning the competence of the sales professional. Recognizing the perils of these pitfalls is the first step towards mastering the art of sales conversations.

Crafting Purposeful Inquiries

Research-Infused Questions: Before engaging in a sales conversation, conduct thorough research on the prospect and their business. Dumb questions often arise when basic information is overlooked. Craft inquiries that reflect your knowledge of their industry, challenges, and goals, demonstrating a genuine interest in their specific situation.

Example: "I noticed your recent expansion into [market]. How has that impacted your [specific aspect] strategy?"

Open-Ended Exploration: Dumb questions often stem from a desire for quick answers rather than a genuine exploration of the prospect's needs. Embrace open-ended questions that invite thoughtful responses, uncovering nuanced insights that can inform your sales approach.

Example: "Can you share more about your current approach to [specific process]? What's working well, and where do you see opportunities for improvement?"

Value-Centric Queries: Questions that solely revolve around the features of your product or service can be perceived as dull and uninspiring. Shift the focus to value by asking about the prospect's goals and aspirations, paving the way for a discussion on how your offering can be a strategic asset.

Example: "In the next quarter, what are the key outcomes you're aiming for? How do you envision our [product/service] contributing to those goals?"

Transforming Mistakes into Opportunities

Acknowledging and Pivoting: Everyone makes mistakes, and acknowledging them gracefully is a mark of professionalism. When you catch yourself asking a less-than-ideal question, pivot seamlessly by providing context or reframing the inquiry to align with the prospect's context.

Example: "I realize that might have been a broad question. Let me narrow it down. Considering [specific aspect], how do you envision our solution fitting into your strategy?"

Learning from Responses: The prospect's responses to your questions offer valuable cues for course correction. Actively listen and adjust your approach based on the information they share. This adaptability not only salvages the conversation but also positions you as an attentive and responsive partner.

Example: "Thank you for sharing your perspective. It helps me understand your priorities better. How can we tailor our solution to align more closely with your objectives?"

The Art of Subtle Guidance

Mastering sales conversations involves a delicate balance between guiding the discussion and allowing the prospect to express their needs. Avoiding dumb questions is not about having a script but about possessing a keen understanding of the prospect's world and using that insight to craft purposeful inquiries.

Embracing Continuous Improvement

The art of crafting compelling questions is a skill that evolves over time. Embrace a mindset of continuous improvement, seeking feedback from successful interactions and learning from questions that didn't yield the desired outcomes. As you refine your approach, each conversation becomes an opportunity for growth and mastery

1. How Are You? - An Automatic Response Trigger

Initiating a conversation with "How are you?" might seem polite, but it triggers a trained automatic response. Instead of progressing the discussion, it often leads to prospects deflecting with a standard "I'm just looking." Learn to open conversations in a way that moves them forward.

Initiating a conversation with the common and seemingly polite question, "How are you?" is a well-established social norm. However, in the realm of sales, this automatic icebreaker triggers a trained response that often hinders the progression of meaningful discussions. In this chapter, we'll explore the limitations of this question and delve into alternative approaches to open conversations that propel them forward.

The Pitfalls of "How Are You?"

Automatic Responses: "How are you?" is a question ingrained in social conventions, leading to automatic responses. In a sales context, this automaticity often results in prospects defaulting to a deflective response, such as "I'm just looking." This leaves the conversation stagnant and fails to provide valuable insights into the prospect's needs.

Lack of Engagement: The question, while well-intentioned, does little to engage the prospect in a meaningful dialogue about their specific challenges, goals, or pain points. It tends to keep the conversation at a surface level, missing the opportunity to uncover crucial information that could inform your sales approach.

Crafting Purposeful Openers

Relevance to Their World: Instead of a generic greeting, tailor your opening to reflect your knowledge of the prospect's industry, recent achievements, or challenges. This immediately signals that your conversation is not a scripted routine but a tailored engagement based on a genuine understanding of their world.

Example: "I noticed your recent expansion into [specific market]. How has that impacted your [relevant aspect] strategy?"

Value-Centric Opening: Begin the conversation by highlighting the value your product or service brings. This shifts the focus from a generic inquiry to a discussion centered around the prospect's needs and the potential solutions you can offer.

Example: "Many of our clients have found that [specific value proposition] significantly improves [relevant outcome]. I'm curious to learn how a similar approach could benefit your [specific area]."

Problem-Solving Approach: Frame your opener as a problem-solving proposition. By addressing a common pain point in the prospect's industry or presenting a solution to a prevalent challenge, you immediately position yourself as a resourceful partner.

Example: "In working with businesses like yours, we often find that [common challenge] is a concern. I'd love to explore how our expertise can help alleviate that pressure for you."

Creating a Dialogue, Not a Transaction

The key to a successful sales conversation lies in creating a dialogue rather than treating it as a transaction. The initial exchange sets the tone for the entire interaction, and a thoughtful opener can pave the way for a more engaging and productive discussion.

Practicing Active Listening

Once the conversation is underway, practice active listening to glean valuable insights. Ask follow-up questions based on the prospect's responses, demonstrating a genuine interest in their unique situation. This not only fosters rapport but also allows you to tailor your sales approach to their specific needs.

2. Are You the Decision Maker? - An Outdated Inquiry

The question of whether someone is the decision maker is not only outdated but also prone to deception. People may lie, whether they have the authority to decide or not. A more effective alternative is asking how decisions of this nature are typically made within their organization.

In the landscape of sales, certain inquiries, while once considered standard, have evolved into outdated relics that often hinder rather than facilitate meaningful conversations. One such question is the direct inquiry of "Are you the decision maker?" This chapter explores the limitations of this outdated question and presents a more effective alternative that navigates potential deception and fosters a more insightful dialogue.

The Pitfalls of "Are You the Decision Maker?"

Prone to Deception: The direct question about decision-making authority can be met with deception. Prospects may misrepresent their level of authority, either to expedite the sales process or to deflect responsibility. This hinders transparency and may lead to misunderstandings later in the sales journey.

Perceived Intrusiveness: The question can be perceived as intrusive, putting the prospect on the defensive. It may create an immediate barrier to open communication, as individuals may feel guarded about revealing their organizational structure or decision-making hierarchy.

Navigating the Inquiry with a Strategic Alternative

Alternative Approach: Inquiring About Decision-Making Process

Instead of directly asking if they are the decision maker, frame the inquiry around understanding how decisions of this nature are typically made within their organization. This alternative not only provides valuable insights into their internal processes but also invites a more collaborative and informative response.

Example: "So that I can better tailor our discussion to meet your organization's needs, could you share with me how decisions around [specific area] are typically made within your team?"

3. So You're Not Interested? - Inviting Conflict

Asking, "So you're not interested?" creates unnecessary conflict and does little to understand the prospect's needs. It positions you as defensive and justifying your value. Rather than assuming disinterest, delve into what challenges or concerns the prospect may have.

The Pitfalls of "So You're Not Interested?"

Inviting Conflict: The direct question about disinterest can be perceived as confrontational, potentially inviting unnecessary conflict. It may put the prospect on the defensive, hindering the possibility of a constructive conversation about their needs or concerns.

Assuming Disinterest: Jumping to the conclusion of disinterest based on a subtle cue may be premature. It positions you as defensive and can lead to misunderstandings. The prospect might have concerns or challenges that need addressing, and assuming disinterest may close the door to uncovering valuable insights.

Shifting the Narrative with a Constructive Alternative

Alternative Approach: Delving into Challenges or Concerns

Instead of assuming disinterest, shift the narrative by expressing a genuine interest in understanding the prospect's perspective. Delve into the challenges or concerns they may have, opening the door to a more nuanced and constructive conversation.

Example: "I sense there might be some concerns or challenges on your end. I'm here to understand and address any specific needs or questions you may have. Could you share more about what's on your mind regarding [specific aspect]?"

4. Are You Ready to Buy Today? - The Threatening Interrogation

Directly asking if the prospect is ready to buy today can be perceived as threatening. It puts them on the defensive and may lead to hesitation or resistance. Opt for more neutral questions that guide the prospect without pressuring them, such as "Where should we go from here?" or "What would you like to do next?"

The Pitfalls of "Are You Ready to Buy Today?"

Perceived Threat: The direct question about immediate readiness to buy can be perceived as a threat. It may create a sense of pressure and put the prospect on the defensive, leading to hesitation or resistance.

Lack of Collaboration: The confrontational nature of the question may hinder collaboration. Sales should be a mutual exploration of value, and an overly direct approach can disrupt the flow of the conversation, impacting the prospect's comfort and openness.

Crafting Neutral and Collaborative Alternatives

Open-Ended Exploration: Opt for open-ended questions that invite the prospect to share their thoughts on the next steps without pressuring them into an immediate decision.

Example: "Given our discussion today, where do you see us going from here?"

Guided Decision-Making: Guide the prospect in considering the next steps without making them feel compelled to decide on the spot.

Example: "What would you like to do next based on our conversation? We have a few options we can explore together."

Understanding Their Perspective: Seek to understand the prospect's perspective on the buying process without insisting on an immediate commitment.

Example: "In your view, what would be the ideal timeline for moving forward, and what factors are most important to you in making this decision?"

Navigating the Decision-Making Landscape

Understanding the prospect's readiness to move forward is crucial, but the approach should be collaborative and non-threatening. By adopting more neutral and open-ended questions, you create a space for the prospect to express their thoughts and preferences without feeling rushed.

5. Can You Afford It? - A Personal Finance Invasion

Inquiring whether the prospect can afford the product or service is intrusive and can create discomfort. Instead of challenging their financial capability, explore ways to provide solutions. Propose options like financing with no interest or breaking down payments to make the purchase more feasible.

The Pitfalls of "Can You Afford It?"

Personal Finance Invasion: Inquiring directly about the prospect's ability to afford the product or service can be perceived as intrusive. It delves into personal financial matters, potentially causing discomfort and hindering the development of a trusting relationship.

Creating Defensiveness: The question may put the prospect on the defensive, as it implies a judgment about their financial situation. This defensive stance can hinder open communication and collaboration in exploring viable solutions.

Offering Empathetic Solutions

Exploring Financing Options: Instead of directly questioning affordability, explore financing options that make the purchase more feasible. This approach shows empathy and a commitment to finding solutions that align with the prospect's financial comfort.

Example: "We offer flexible financing options, including no-interest plans. This way, you can choose a payment plan that fits comfortably within your budget. Would you like more details on these options?"

Breaking Down Payments: Propose breaking down the total cost into manageable payments. This not only addresses affordability concerns but also demonstrates your willingness to work collaboratively with the prospect.

Example: "To make it more convenient for you, we can break down the total cost into monthly payments. How does that sound in terms of fitting into your budget?"

Empathetic Inquiry: Instead of assuming financial constraints, approach the topic with empathy. Ask open-ended questions that allow the prospect to share their preferences and concerns without feeling pressured.

Example: "I understand everyone has unique financial considerations. What factors are most important to you when making a purchase decision, and how can we tailor our approach to meet your needs?"

6. Are You Saying You Don't Have the Power? - Offensive and Rude

Questioning the prospect's decision-making power is not only offensive but also counterproductive. Whether they can or cannot make decisions independently, the question is bound to yield unhelpful responses. Focus on understanding their decision-making process and involvement in the purchase.

The Pitfalls of "Do You Have the Power?"

Offensive and Rude: Directly questioning the prospect's decision-making power can be offensive. It may come across as rude and disrespectful, potentially damaging the rapport built during the conversation.

Unhelpful Responses: Whether the prospect can or cannot make decisions independently, the question is likely to yield unhelpful responses. It puts the prospect on the defensive and may lead to unproductive and defensive conversations.

Navigating Decision-Making Dynamics with Respect

Understanding Decision-Making Processes: Instead of challenging the prospect's authority, focus on understanding the decision-making processes within their organization. This approach allows you to gather valuable insights without causing discomfort.

Example: "Could you provide insights into how decisions like this are typically made within your team or organization? This will help me tailor our discussion to align with your process."

Involvement in the Purchase: Inquire about the prospect's role and level of involvement in the purchase without questioning their decision-making power directly.

Example: "I'm curious about your role in this purchase. How do you envision your involvement, and are there other key stakeholders I should be aware of?"

Collaborative Exploration: Frame questions in a way that invites collaboration rather than challenging authority. This fosters a more positive and open discussion about decision-making.

Example: "As we move forward, how can we collaborate to ensure that all decision-makers are informed and comfortable with the process?"

7. When Should I Call You Back? - A Defensive Tactic

The question of when to call back puts you in a defensive position, assuming the prospect needs time to think. Instead, gain clarity on the specific timeframe and what additional information or support they require during that period.

The Pitfalls of "When Should I Call You Back?"

Defensive Positioning: The question of when to call back can position you defensively, assuming the prospect needs time to think. This may create distance and hinder the momentum built during the conversation.

Assuming Time is the Only Factor: The question may assume that time is the sole consideration for the prospect. It overlooks the possibility that additional information or support may be needed during the decision-making process.

Proactive and Engaging Alternatives

Gaining Clarity on Timeframe: Instead of assuming the need for time, inquire about the prospect's specific timeframe for making a decision. This proactive approach demonstrates your commitment to aligning with their timeline.

Example: "I understand decisions like this take time. Could you share your preferred timeframe for making a decision, so I can ensure our follow-up is timely and supportive?"

Identifying Information or Support Needs: Explore whether the prospect requires additional information or support during the decision-making process. This not only addresses their specific needs but also positions you as a valuable resource.

Example: "As you consider your decision, is there any specific information or support you would find helpful? Our goal is to ensure you have everything you need to make an informed choice."

Tailoring Follow-Up to Their Preferences: Inquire about the prospect's preferred mode of communication and frequency for follow-ups. This tailored approach respects their preferences and enhances the overall experience.

Example: "To make our follow-up more convenient for you, could you share your preferred mode of communication and how often you'd like updates on our progress?"

Mastering Objections – Navigating the "What If It Doesn't Work?" Dilemma

In the fast-paced world of sales, objections are the battleground where deals are won or lost. Today, we delve into a common objection: "What if it doesn't work?" Explore the strategies to handle this concern with finesse and turn objections into opportunities.

Lights, Camera, Action: The Constant Filming Mentality

In the realm of sales, every moment is an opportunity. The chapter begins with a reminder to keep the camera rolling, capturing the essence of interactions. Except for bathroom breaks, let the lens be a silent witness to the art of closing deals.

The Cinematic Metaphor

Every Moment is a Scene: In the film of sales, every moment presents a scene laden with potential. Whether it's the initial greeting, the exploration of needs, or the grand finale of closing, each interaction contributes to the narrative of success.

Crafting Your Storyline: Embrace the role of both director and actor in this cinematic journey. Craft a compelling storyline that resonates with your audience—the prospects. Be intentional in shaping each scene to build anticipation and leave a lasting impression.

The Art of Opening Credits

Strategic Greetings and Introductions: The opening credits set the tone for the entire film. Ensure your greetings and introductions are not just routine but strategic. Capture attention from the start, making your prospect eager to see what unfolds.

Example: "Welcome to the premiere of tailored solutions designed just for you. I'm thrilled to have you as the lead in this production."

Establishing the Setting: Clearly define the setting of your film—your brand and the value it brings. Set the stage for the prospect to visualize the story unfolding in a space where their needs are met and challenges overcome.

Example: "Picture this: a world where your challenges find solutions, and your goals take center stage. That's the setting we've crafted for our collaboration."

The Art of Scene Development

Exploring Needs as Plot Points: Each interaction that delves into the prospect's needs is a crucial plot point. Dive deep into their challenges and aspirations, using these insights to develop the plot of your collaborative journey.

Example: "Let's explore the plot twists together—your challenges and aspirations. How can we sculpt a storyline that leads to your desired outcome?"

Dialogue as Script: Your dialogue becomes the script that guides the narrative. Choose your words with precision, ensuring they align with the overarching story you're telling—the story of value and solutions.

Example: "Every word we exchange is a line from the script of success. Let's ensure each dialogue resonates with the prospect's aspirations."

The Grand Finale: Closing Scenes

Building to the Climax: As you approach the closing scenes, build momentum to the climax. Clearly articulate the value proposition and how your solution is the resolution they've been waiting for.

Example: "Now, as we approach the final scenes, let's magnify the value. Imagine the climax of achieving your goals with our tailored solution."

Sealing the Deal as the Closing Credits Roll: The closing scenes are where the magic happens. Seal the deal with finesse, leaving a lasting impression as the closing credits begin to roll.

Example: "It's time to wrap up this production with a bang. As the closing credits roll, envision the success that awaits with our partnership."

The Takeaway: Strategic Reflection

The "Constant Filming Mentality" urges you to view each sales encounter as a scene in your cinematic journey. Strategically reflect on your performance, identifying areas for improvement and celebrating the scenes where you shine. The film of your sales career is a dynamic production, and with each scene, you have the opportunity to captivate your audience and leave a lasting impact.

Agent Leaders and Objection Handling: A Collaborative Approach

The discussion shifts to the role of agent leaders in managing objections. An objection that surfaces is the fear of the product or service not delivering as promised. This chapter aims to equip agent leaders with effective responses to address this concern and instill confidence in prospects.

Role-Playing Dynamics: Unraveling Objections Through Scenarios

Engage in a dynamic role play where objection handling takes center stage. The prospect expresses apprehension: "What if it doesn't work?" The closer responds, emphasizing the importance of understanding the prospect's definition of success.

Understanding the Fear: "What if it doesn't work?"

Unpacking Apprehension: The prospect's fear of the product or service not meeting expectations is a common objection. Agent leaders must first empathize with this concern, acknowledging the prospect's apprehension.

Example: "I appreciate your honesty. It's completely normal to have concerns about whether our solution will align with your expectations. Let's explore that together."

Role-Playing Dynamics: Engage in dynamic role-playing scenarios where objection handling takes center stage. Through these exercises, agent leaders can refine their responses and foster a collaborative approach to addressing objections.

Role Play Scenario: Emphasizing Success Alignment

Prospect: "What if it doesn't work?"

Closer (Agent Leader): "I completely understand your concern. The success of our collaboration is of utmost importance. To address this, let's explore what success looks like for you. Can you share specific outcomes or milestones that would define a successful partnership from your perspective?"

Strategies for Agent Leaders:

Define Success Together: Redirect the conversation toward defining success collaboratively. This not only addresses the prospect's concern but also aligns expectations and sets the stage for a more tailored solution.

Example Response: "Let's work together to define what success means for you. By understanding your specific goals and expectations, we can ensure our solution is not only effective but tailored to your unique needs."

Highlight Customization and Flexibility: Emphasize the flexibility and customization of your offerings. Assure the prospect that the solution can be adapted to meet their evolving needs, mitigating the fear of a one-size-fits-all approach.

Example Response: "Our approach is highly flexible, and we understand that your needs may evolve. Our commitment is to customize our solution to align with your changing requirements, ensuring ongoing success."

Provide Case Studies and Success Stories: Share relevant case studies and success stories that showcase the positive outcomes experienced by similar clients. This provides tangible evidence of the product or service delivering on its promises.

Example Response: "Let me share a case study with you where we helped a client facing similar concerns. The success they achieved might resonate with your goals, and we can apply similar strategies to ensure your success."

Strategies for Overcoming Objections: A Closer's Arsenal

1. Define Expectations Clearly

When faced with the objection, inquire about the prospect's definition of success. What results are they anticipating? By clarifying expectations, the closer gains a precise understanding of the prospect's goals.

2. Addressing Past Experiences

Objections often stem from past negative experiences. Skillfully probe the prospect's history with similar products or services. Uncover emotional baggage and address concerns related to previous disappointments.

3. The Direct Approach

For those armed with confidence, a direct approach can be employed. Responding to "What if it doesn't work?" with "What if it does?" injects a dose of optimism and redirects the conversation towards potential success.

Strategy 1: Define Expectations Clearly

Approach: When faced with the objection, inquire about the prospect's definition of success. What results are they anticipating? By clarifying expectations, the closer gains a precise understanding of the prospect's goals.

Example Response: "I appreciate your concern. To ensure our collaboration meets your expectations, could you share more about what success looks like for you? What specific outcomes or milestones are you hoping to achieve?"

Strategy 2: Addressing Past Experiences

Approach: Objections often stem from past negative experiences. Skillfully probe the prospect's history with similar products or services. Uncover emotional baggage and address concerns related to previous disappointments.

Example Response: "I sense there might be concerns based on past experiences. Could you share more about your previous interactions with similar solutions? Understanding your history will help us tailor our approach to address those specific concerns."

Strategy 3: The Direct Approach

Approach: For those armed with confidence, a direct approach can be employed. Responding to "What if it doesn't work?" with "What if it does?" injects a dose of optimism and redirects the conversation towards potential success.

Example Response: "I hear your concern, and it's valid to consider all possibilities. However, what if our solution exceeds your expectations and brings the success you're aiming for? Let's explore the positive outcomes that await us."

Strategy 4: Collaborative Problem-Solving

Approach: Engage the prospect in collaborative problem-solving. Position the objection as a challenge to overcome together, showcasing your commitment to working closely with them.

Example Response: "I appreciate your honesty, and I see this as an opportunity for us to work together closely. Let's dive into the specifics of your concerns and collaboratively develop a plan to ensure our solution aligns perfectly with your needs."

CHAPTER THIRTEEN

Virtual Mastery – Unveiling the Art of Closing

In the dynamic landscape of modern business, learning the art of closing has evolved into a virtual endeavor. In this chapter, we explore a revolutionary methodology developed by a seasoned mentor, focusing on the four crucial stages of mastering the closing game.

The Four Stages of Closing Mastery

1. Learn It: Foundational Principles

Embarking on the journey of closing starts with acquiring the fundamental principles. Whether through traditional methods or the school of hard knocks, grasping the basics is the initial step toward becoming a proficient closer.

The Traditional Classroom:

Understanding the Sales Funnel: Begin with a deep dive into the sales funnel, understanding the stages from prospecting to closing. Recognize the significance of each stage and how they interconnect to guide prospects through the buying journey.

Mastering Communication Skills: Communication is the backbone of successful sales. Learn the art of active listening, effective questioning, and persuasive dialogue. These skills lay the groundwork for building strong relationships with prospects.

Product and Industry Knowledge: Becoming a subject matter expert is crucial. Invest time in understanding your product or service inside out, as well as staying abreast of industry trends. This knowledge builds credibility and enhances your ability to address prospect concerns.

The School of Hard Knocks:

Learning from Rejections: Rejections are not setbacks but invaluable lessons. Embrace them as opportunities to refine your approach. Analyze the reasons behind rejections and use them to adapt and improve your strategy.

Experiencing Varied Sales Scenarios: Closing is a dynamic skill, and exposure to diverse sales scenarios is essential. Navigate different objections, handle challenging prospects, and immerse yourself in a variety of sales situations to broaden your skill set.

Mentorship and Shadowing: Learn from those who have mastered the art of closing. Seek mentorship opportunities or shadow successful closers to observe their techniques, strategies, and the nuances of their approach.

The Fusion of Learning Approaches:

Continuous Learning: The journey of closing is ongoing. Stay committed to continuous learning by staying informed about industry changes, adopting new sales technologies, and refining your skills based on evolving market dynamics.

Adaptability and Flexibility: The closing landscape is ever-changing. Cultivate adaptability and flexibility in your approach. Be open to trying new strategies, incorporating feedback, and adjusting your methods based on the unique needs of each prospect.

Building Resilience: Resilience is a fundamental trait of successful closers. Learn to bounce back from setbacks, rejections, and challenges. Develop a mindset that views obstacles as opportunities for growth.

2. Understand It: Unraveling the "Why"

Mere knowledge is insufficient; understanding the underlying principles is imperative. Drawing parallels with martial arts, the chapter highlights the importance of comprehending the rationale behind each closing technique. This deeper understanding forms the groundwork for mastery.

The Martial Arts Analogy:

The Importance of Technique: In martial arts, every move has a purpose. Similarly, in closing, each technique serves a distinct purpose. Understanding why a particular technique is employed allows closers to execute with precision and intention.

Efficiency in Execution: Martial artists don't merely memorize movements; they understand the biomechanics and strategy behind each technique. Similarly, closers who grasp the "why" behind their methods operate with efficiency, maximizing the impact of their actions.

Adaptability in Dynamic Situations: In martial arts, adaptability is crucial. Understanding the principles enables practitioners to adapt techniques to varying situations. Similarly, closers who comprehend the rationale behind their methods can navigate diverse scenarios with finesse.

Unraveling the "Why" in Closing:

Building Trust and Rapport: Why is building trust essential in closing? Understanding that trust is the foundation of successful relationships with prospects allows closers to prioritize authenticity and connection.

Handling Objections Effectively: Why address objections in a specific way? Understanding that objections are opportunities for clarification and collaboration empowers closers to handle objections with confidence and finesse.

Creating a Sense of Urgency: Why introduce urgency in closing? Recognizing that urgency can propel prospects to take action allows closers to strategically guide the decision-making process and avoid procrastination.

The Fusion of Knowledge and Understanding:

Strategic Application of Techniques: Knowledge provides a repertoire of techniques, but understanding the "why" enables closers to strategically apply these techniques based on the unique dynamics of each sales interaction.

Continuous Refinement: With a deep understanding of the principles, closers can continually refine their approach. Each encounter becomes an opportunity to apply knowledge in a nuanced way, adapting to the specific needs of the prospect.

3. Master It: The Power of Practice

To reach the mastery stage, relentless practice is key. The chapter advocates for the use of role play, creating simulated sales scenarios for learners to navigate. The global role play platform becomes the verbal dojo, allowing students to spar verbally, enhancing their skills in a safe environment.

The Verbal Dojo: Where Mastery Takes Shape

Purposeful Practice: In martial arts, practitioners engage in purposeful practice to refine their techniques. Similarly, closers must immerse themselves in purposeful practice, using every interaction as an opportunity to enhance their skills.

Role Play as a Training Ground: The chapter emphasizes role play as the training ground for mastering closing techniques. Creating simulated sales scenarios allows learners to navigate objections, handle diverse prospects, and fine-tune their approaches in a controlled environment.

The Global Role Play Platform: Introducing the concept of a global role play platform, this chapter envisions a space where learners from around the world can engage in virtual sparring sessions. This platform becomes the verbal dojo, enabling learners to practice with peers, receive feedback, and elevate their skills collaboratively.

Advantages of Role Play:

Realistic Scenarios: Role play replicates real-life scenarios, providing closers with the opportunity to encounter objections, resistance, and diverse personalities in a controlled setting.

Feedback and Improvement: The verbal dojo allows learners to receive constructive feedback from peers and mentors. This feedback loop is instrumental in identifying areas for improvement and refining closing techniques.

Building Confidence: Practice builds confidence. Engaging in role play consistently enhances closers' confidence in handling objections, guiding conversations, and ultimately, closing deals.

Navigating the Verbal Dojo:

Diverse Scenarios for Mastery: The global role play platform features diverse scenarios, ensuring that learners encounter a spectrum of challenges. From objections to negotiations, each sparring session contributes to mastery.

Peer Collaboration: Learners collaborate with peers, sharing insights and strategies. The global nature of the platform introduces a variety of perspectives, enriching the learning experience.

Continuous Improvement: Mastery is a journey of continuous improvement. The verbal dojo serves as a dynamic space where closers refine their skills, adapt to evolving market dynamics, and stay at the forefront of their craft.

4. Forget It: Unconscious Competence

True mastery is attained when one can execute closing techniques effortlessly and unconsciously. This stage involves transcending scripts and allowing the conversation to flow naturally. The seasoned closer can anticipate the prospect's responses several moves ahead, creating a seamless interaction.

Unconscious Competence: The Apex of Mastery

Effortless Execution: At the stage of unconscious competence, closing techniques are executed with ease. Closers seamlessly integrate their skills into conversations without the need for conscious thought or reliance on predetermined scripts.

Natural Flow of Conversation: Conversations flow organically, unencumbered by the need to consciously recall techniques or responses. The seasoned closer effortlessly navigates objections, guides discussions, and builds rapport, allowing the natural rhythm of the conversation to take center stage.

Anticipation of Prospect Responses: A hallmark of unconscious competence is the ability to anticipate the prospect's responses. The seasoned closer can intuitively gauge the prospect's reactions, foresee potential objections, and strategically navigate the conversation several moves ahead.

Transcending Scripts:

Intuitive Adaptation: Unconscious competence involves intuitive adaptation to the prospect's cues. Closers no longer rely on rigid scripts but effortlessly tailor their approach based on the unique dynamics of each interaction.

Authentic Connection: Authenticity becomes a hallmark of the seasoned closer. The ability to connect with prospects on a genuine level, free from the constraints of memorized responses, fosters trust and strengthens client relationships.

Dynamic Problem-Solving: Challenges are met with dynamic problem-solving. Unconscious competence empowers closers to navigate unforeseen obstacles seamlessly, relying on a deep understanding of closing principles rather than prescriptive solutions.

The Journey to Mastery:

Progression Through Stages: Mastery in closing is a progression through stages—from conscious incompetence to conscious competence, then to unconscious competence. Each stage represents a level of refinement and skill acquisition.

Continuous Learning and Adaptation: Even at the stage of unconscious competence, the seasoned closer remains committed to continuous learning and adaptation. The dynamic nature of sales requires ongoing refinement and staying attuned to industry shifts.

Analyzing the Role-Play Dialogue: Navigating the Experience Inquiry

In this role-play dialogue, the instructor, assuming the role of a digital marketing service provider, engages in a conversation with a prospect who is concerned about the provider's level of experience. The interaction provides a practical example of handling a common objection in sales.

Emphasize Expertise Over Years:

Clients often inquire about experience to gauge your expertise and competence. Instead of merely stating the number of years you've been in the industry, shift the focus to your expertise and the value you bring to the table.

Example: "While I have been in the industry for five years, what truly sets me apart is the depth of experience I've gained in solving challenges similar to yours. In my previous role, I successfully implemented strategies that resulted in a 20% increase in client satisfaction within the first year."

Highlight Relevant Achievements:

Rather than providing a generic answer, tailor your response to highlight achievements and successes that are relevant to the client's needs. This not only addresses their concerns about experience but also demonstrates the practical application of your skills.

Example: "In my three years of experience, I've had the privilege of working on projects similar to yours. For instance, in my last role, I led a team that increased revenue by 30% through a targeted marketing campaign. I'm confident that I can leverage this experience to drive results for your business as well."

Showcase Continuous Learning:

Acknowledge the importance of staying current in a rapidly evolving industry. Mention any certifications, training programs, or professional development initiatives you've undertaken. This communicates your commitment to staying at the forefront of industry trends.

Example: "In my eight years in this field, I've not only accumulated hands-on experience but have also prioritized continuous learning. I recently completed a certification in the latest industry technologies, ensuring that I bring cutting-edge solutions to my clients."

Relate Experience to Client Needs:

Connect your experience directly to the client's needs. Explain how your background positions you to understand and address their specific challenges, reinforcing the idea that your experience is an asset tailored to their requirements.

Example: "My decade-long experience has equipped me to understand the intricacies of the challenges your industry faces. For instance, in my previous role, I navigated a similar market shift successfully, and I believe this experience positions me well to guide your business through similar transitions."

Leverage Testimonials and Success Stories:

Bring in social proof by referencing testimonials or success stories from previous clients or colleagues. This not only validates your experience but also provides tangible evidence of your ability to deliver results.

Example: "Over the years, I've had the privilege of working with diverse clients, and their feedback speaks to the impact of my expertise. One client commended my strategic approach, noting a 25% increase in customer engagement after implementing my recommendations."

Express Enthusiasm and Adaptability:

Even if you have limited experience in a specific area, express enthusiasm and a willingness to adapt and learn. Emphasize your ability to bring fresh perspectives and innovative solutions to the client's challenges.

Example: "While I may be relatively new to this industry, my background in XYZ has equipped me with transferable skills such as data analysis and strategic planning. I'm eager to bring a fresh perspective to your team and am confident in my ability to quickly adapt and contribute."

Key Takeaways:

Acknowledging Commonality:

The instructor starts by acknowledging that the prospect's question about experience is common, immediately establishing a relatable tone.

Proposal for Role-Play:

A dynamic approach is introduced as the instructor suggests a role-play scenario, making the learning experience more interactive.

Transparent Conversation:

The prospect poses the experience question, and the instructor responds with curiosity, seeking to understand the underlying concern rather than immediately defending their experience.

Addressing Past Mistakes:

The prospect shares past negative experiences with hiring and financial losses, creating an opportunity for the instructor to navigate these concerns.

Transparency and Honesty:

The instructor openly admits to a lack of extensive experience but refrains from defensive responses. Instead, the focus is shifted to understanding the prospect's needs and offering a commitment to hard work.

Understanding Prospect's Motivation:

Through skillful questioning, the instructor uncovers the prospect's motivations and challenges, laying the foundation for a more personalized pitch.

Avoiding Overpromising:

The instructor reassures the prospect by avoiding overpromising and emphasizing the uniqueness of each client. This builds credibility and manages the prospect's expectations.

Value Proposition:

Rather than guaranteeing specific results, the instructor shifts the conversation towards adding value to the prospect's business model and offers a collaborative approach.

Empathetic Communication:

Empathy is woven into the conversation, acknowledging the prospect's hesitations and presenting a solution-oriented discussion.

Encouraging Results-Based Decision:

The prospect expresses a preference for results, and the instructor aligns with this by emphasizing a results-based approach.

Comparisons to Personal Experience:

The instructor draws on personal experiences as a young copywriter to demonstrate the commitment to hard work and dedication, providing a relatable example.

Encouragement for Further Learning:

The role-play concludes with encouragement for the student to share this scenario with others, enhancing the learning experience.

Bonus Testimonials:

The video includes snippets of successful closings by HTC family members, adding a motivational element to the content.

Call-to-Action for Additional Learning:

The video concludes with a call-to-action, inviting viewers to access a free training series for more role-play scenarios and insights into effective closing strategies.

CHAPTER FIFTEEN

Mastering the Art of Three-Options Strategy: The Middle Option Advantage

Are you eager to boost your sales and encourage customers to make purchases more frequently? Today, we'll delve into a simple yet powerful sales technique that has proven effective across various industries. This technique revolves around an age-old concept known as "The Boxes."

The Power of Choice:

When it comes to selling a product or service, customers are often presented with a binary decision – to buy or not to buy. This leaves them pondering affordability and budget constraints, focusing primarily on price.

Introducing "The Boxes":

The magic happens when you introduce choices. Think back to the days of ordering sodas at a movie theater. You had two options – a large or a small. Statistics showed that 70% opted for the small, playing it safe to save money. But then, a third choice was introduced.

The Three-Box Strategy:

Picture three soda sizes – small, regular (formerly large), and the jumbo-sized drink. This creates what we call "contrast pricing." The key is to position your offers strategically, making one option too extravagant, another too basic, and the middle one, the sweet spot.

Consumer Psychology:

With three choices, consumers shift from a binary decision (buy or don't buy) to a more nuanced one (which one to buy). It taps into psychology, making the decision-making process more engaging and less focused on a simple yes or no.

Contrast Pricing in Action:

Apply this strategy to your business by creating three distinct offers. Make the high-end offer extravagant, the low-end offer basic, and the middle one – the one you truly want to sell – compelling. This ensures your customers are guided towards the middle choice.

Real-Life Examples:

Explore how businesses implement the three-box strategy. For instance, a car wash might offer a basic exterior shampoo for $20, an enhanced version with interior vacuuming for $25, and a full detailing package for $50. The middle option becomes the irresistible choice for most customers.

Balancing Choices:

While the three-box strategy works wonders, offering too many choices can lead to confusion. Four or more options might overwhelm customers. Keep it simple, with three well-crafted choices.

Decoy Pricing:

Understand that the extravagant offer isn't meant to be the primary seller. It serves as a decoy, capturing the attention of a niche market willing to pay a premium. The majority of your customers, ideally, should find the middle option most appealing.

In the symphony of sales, the strategic use of three options can orchestrate harmony between customer preferences and business objectives. This chapter delves into the brilliance of the three-options strategy, unveiling how positioning the middle option as the best value can become a game-changer across diverse industries.

Understanding the Three-Options Strategy:

The three-options strategy is more than a pricing structure; it's a psychological dance that guides customers toward a predetermined choice. It involves presenting three choices: a basic option, a premium option, and strategically, the middle option positioned as the best value. This approach leverages the psychology of decision-making, nudging customers towards the option that the business desires.

Soft Drink Purchase in Theatres: A Classic Example:

Think about the last time you visited a movie theater. When it comes to soft drinks, you're presented with three options: Small, Medium, and Large. The Medium, in this scenario, is strategically priced and sized to appear as the best value. It's not too small that it seems insufficient, and it's not too large that it feels extravagant. The Medium option is designed to be just right, appealing to the majority of customers.

Translating the Strategy Across Industries:

1. Gym Memberships:

a) Basic Membership (Access to Equipment):

- Standard Gym Access
- General Equipment Use

b) Premium Membership (Best Value):

- All Basic Features
- Access to Group Classes
- Personalized Training Plan

c) VIP Membership (Premium Features):

- All Premium Features
- 24/7 Access
- Exclusive Classes and Events

Explanation: The Premium Membership, strategically placed as the best value, offers a comprehensive fitness experience with added perks, making it the ideal choice for fitness enthusiasts.

2. Software Subscriptions:

a) Basic Plan (Limited Features):

- Essential Features
- Standard Customer Support

b) Standard Plan (Best Value):

- More Features
- Priority Customer Support
- Access to Webinars and Tutorials

c) Premium Plan (Premium Features):

- All Standard Features

- Advanced Analytics
- Dedicated Account Manager

Explanation: The Standard Plan is positioned as the best value, providing a balanced set of features with enhanced support and learning resources, making it the preferred choice for users.

3. Car Wash Services:

a) Basic Wash (Exterior Only):

- Standard Exterior Cleaning
- Air Dry

b) Deluxe Wash (Best Value):

- Exterior and Interior Cleaning
- Hand Dry
- Tire Shine

c) Premium Wash (Premium Features):

- All Deluxe Features
- Wax Coating
- Interior Detailing

Explanation: The Deluxe Wash is strategically presented as the best value, offering a comprehensive cleaning package with added features, making it the preferred choice for customers seeking a thorough car cleaning.

Why Does the Middle Option Shine?

Perceived Value: The middle option is strategically crafted to provide a sense of balance, offering more than the basic option but not overwhelming customers with unnecessary features.

Decision Simplicity: Customers are presented with a clear and straightforward decision-making process. The middle option is often perceived as the "sweet spot" between too little and too much.

Majority Appeal: Positioned as the best value, the middle option tends to resonate with the majority of customers, making it a popular choice.

Implementing the Strategy in Your Business:

Know Your Customers:

Understand the preferences and priorities of your target audience. What features or benefits are most appealing to them?

Craft Options Thoughtfully:

Ensure that each option serves a purpose. The basic option should cater to minimal needs, the premium option should offer exclusivity, and the middle option should strike a balance.

Price Strategically:

Price the middle option competitively. It should be perceived as a great deal, providing enhanced value without breaking the bank.

Highlight the Value Proposition:

Clearly communicate why the middle option is the best value. What additional benefits does it offer? Why is it the optimal choice?

Conclusion: Elevate Your Sales Symphony with the Three-Options Strategy:

The art of presenting three options, with the middle option strategically positioned as the best value, is a powerful tool in the hands of a savvy business. By understanding the psychology of consumer decision-making and tailoring options to meet customer needs, businesses can orchestrate a symphony of sales success across various industries. The three-options strategy isn't just about choices; it's about guiding customers towards a decision that aligns with both their desires and the business's objectives.

CHAPTER SIXTEEN

Analysis of the Role-Play Dialogue: Addressing Financial Concerns and Decision-Making Dynamics

Acknowledge and Respect: Start by acknowledging and respecting their need to consult with their spouse. This shows empathy and understanding of the importance of joint decision-making.

Example: *"I completely understand the significance of making decisions together. It's important to have everyone on the same page, especially for something as significant as this."

Reassure and Provide Information: Reassure the client that you're here to provide any additional information or clarification that might help in their discussion. Offer to address any concerns or questions they or their spouse might have.

Example: *"I want to ensure that both you and your spouse feel confident in this decision. If there's any information or clarification that would be helpful for your discussion, please let me know. I'm here to assist in any way."

Share Success Stories: Share success stories or testimonials of other clients who were initially hesitant but found value in your product or service. This can help build confidence and showcase positive outcomes.

Example: *"Many of our clients initially had reservations, but after discussing the benefits with their spouses, they found that our solution brought tremendous value. I'd be happy to share some success stories that might resonate with you both."

Offer a Follow-Up: Propose a follow-up meeting or call to address any concerns or questions they or their spouse might have after their discussion. This demonstrates your commitment to their decision-making process.

Example: *"I completely understand the need to consult with your spouse. How about we schedule a follow-up call to address any questions that may arise during your discussion? I'm here to make sure you both feel comfortable and informed."

Create a Joint Discussion: If appropriate, suggest a joint discussion where you can speak directly to both parties. This can facilitate open communication and provide an opportunity for everyone to express their concerns or questions.

Example: *"If it would be helpful, I'm more than happy to join a call or meeting with both you and your spouse. This way, we can ensure that all questions are addressed, and everyone is on the same page."

Express Understanding of Budget Concerns: If the objection is related to budget concerns, express empathy and offer flexibility. Assure them that you're willing to work within their financial parameters.

Example: *"I understand that budget considerations are crucial. Let's discuss any budget constraints openly, and I'll do my best to tailor a solution that aligns with your financial goals."

Scenario: Overcoming Financial Hesitation in Property Purchase and Involving the Spouse

Setting: Raj, a potential homebuyer, is interested in purchasing a property but is hesitant due to financial concerns. The real estate agent initiates a conversation to understand Raj's motivations and address his reservations.

Agent (Amit): Hi Raj, I noticed you've been exploring properties in this area. What sparked your interest?

Raj: Well, I've been thinking about buying a property for a while now, and I came across this one. It looks great, but I'm a bit hesitant about the financial aspect.

Agent (Amit): I completely understand, Raj. Real estate is a significant investment. Can you tell me more about what's causing the hesitation?

Raj: It's a substantial amount of money, and I want to make sure it fits within our budget. I need to discuss it with my wife, Meera, before making any commitments.

Agent (Amit): Family discussions are crucial in such decisions. How long have you and Meera been considering buying a property?

Raj: We've been married for about 6 years now.

Agent (Amit): Great. When you discuss this property with Meera, how do you think she might respond?

Raj: She might say it's a significant financial commitment. We both want to be cautious and ensure we make the right decision.

Agent (Amit): Completely understandable. What if we set up a call with both of you? We can discuss any questions or concerns Meera might have directly. How does that sound?

Raj: That could work. I've tried involving her by showing her pictures, but maybe a direct conversation could help.

Agent (Amit): Excellent. Let's schedule a three-way call. During the call, we can address any questions and ensure you both feel comfortable with the decision. What time tomorrow works for you?

Raj: Tomorrow at 4 p.m. would be convenient.

Agent (Amit): Perfect. I'll be available. Remember, the purpose of the call is not to pressure Meera but to provide information and answer any questions. We want to make sure you both feel confident about this property. Deal?

Raj: Deal. Thanks a lot for your assistance.

End of Scenario

In this scenario, the real estate agent, Amit, successfully engages with Raj, understanding his motivations and addressing financial concerns related to property purchase. By suggesting a three-way call with Meera, Amit ensures open communication and involvement of all decision-makers. This approach aims to build trust, provide clarity, and facilitate a joint decision-making process in the context of real estate.

CHAPTER SEVENTEEN

The Art of Pre-Selling

Imagine a world where you could seal the deal before even reaching the end of your presentation. What if your prospects were so captivated by your product or service that they were ready to buy before you even mentioned features and benefits? Intriguing, isn't it? In this chapter, we'll explore the transformative power of pre-selling, a game-changing strategy that can redefine your approach to closing sales.

At the heart of this concept lies a fundamental truth—one that challenges the conventional belief that the close happens only at the end of the sale. The real close, I argue, occurs long before that, during what I like to call the pre-selling phase. It's the period when a prospect first reaches out via email, fills out an application form, or schedules a call. This is where the foundation of trust is laid, setting the stage for a successful close.

Let's delve into two scenarios to illustrate the significance of pre-selling. In the first scenario, picture a search engine optimization (SEO) company making cold calls, pitching their services without prior engagement. It's a classic case of selling without pre-selling. The potential client may have a need, but trust is lacking, hindering the likelihood of a successful sale.

Now, shift your focus to the second scenario—a similar SEO company, but with a robust online presence. They share valuable content, showcase client success stories, maintain an active social media presence, and even offer free audits or reports. By the time a prospect engages with this company, trust has already been established through the content they've consumed.

The key takeaway is clear: the more value you provide upfront, the easier it becomes to close the sale. It's not just about having excellent closing skills; it's about strategically pre-selling before you even enter the sales conversation.

But what if you find yourself representing a company that lacks the necessary content, testimonials, or a strong online presence? Closing for such companies is undoubtedly more challenging. Skepticism runs high, and the road to a successful close is steep. This emphasizes the importance of choosing the right company to represent or, if you're a business owner, dedicating ample time to both pre-selling and selling.

Closing at the beginning of a call, also known as the "upfront close," involves setting the tone for a productive conversation right from the start. While a traditional close typically occurs at the end of a sales pitch, closing at the beginning aims to establish commitment and engagement early on. Here are some strategies to effectively close at the beginning of a call:

Establish Clear Objectives: Before the call, define clear objectives and outcomes you aim to achieve. Whether it's scheduling a follow-up meeting, obtaining specific information, or securing commitment, having a clear goal will guide your approach.

Start with a Positive Affirmation: Begin the call on a positive note by expressing appreciation or enthusiasm. This sets a friendly tone and lays the foundation for a cooperative conversation.

Example:

"Thank you for taking the time to speak with me today. I'm excited about our conversation."

State Your Intentions Clearly: Articulate the purpose of the call upfront. Clearly communicate what you hope to accomplish, and be concise to capture the prospect's attention.

Example:

"The main goal of our call today is to explore how our solution can address [specific pain point] and determine if it's a good fit for your needs."

Ask for Commitment to Time: Secure commitment to the allotted time for the call. This reinforces the importance of the conversation and sets the expectation for an engaged and focused discussion.

Example:

"I appreciate your time today. I've set aside [specific amount of time] to ensure we cover everything thoroughly. Does that work for you?"

Probe for Initial Agreement: Introduce a question or statement that prompts the prospect to express agreement or alignment with your objectives. This early agreement creates a sense of collaboration.

Example:

"Would you agree that finding a solution to [specific challenge] is a priority for your team right now?"

Use assumptive language: Employ assumptive language to subtly guide the prospect toward a positive response. This technique involves framing statements in a way that assumes agreement or commitment.

Example:

"As we discuss how our product can streamline your processes, I'm confident you'll see the value it brings to your team."

Provide a Preview of Value: Offer a brief preview of the value or benefits the prospect can expect from the conversation. Highlighting the potential gains piques their interest and encourages active participation.

Example:

"During our call, I'll share insights on how our solution has helped similar companies increase efficiency by [specific percentage]."

Transition Smoothly into the Agenda: After securing commitment and setting a positive tone, smoothly transition into the agenda for the call. Outline the topics you'll cover, ensuring alignment with the prospect's needs and interests.

Example:

"Now that we're aligned on our goals for this call, let me walk you through the agenda. We'll start by discussing [topic], then move on to [next topic], and conclude with [final topic]."

Handling the 'Work for Free' Objection with Finesse

In the rough and tumble world of business, the request to work for free can be a jarring experience. It's a scenario many entrepreneurs and sales professionals encounter, often leaving them wondering how to navigate this tricky situation. In this chapter, we'll explore strategies to handle the "work for free" objection with finesse, turning a potential hurdle into an opportunity for a successful close.

When faced with such a proposition, it's tempting to respond with frustration or dismissal. However, as we'll discuss, there's a more strategic and refined approach—one that employs the key word of the day: finesse.

Firstly, finesse, in this context, is about redirecting rather than confronting. Picture it as a graceful Tai Chi move—a strategic sidestep to address the objection without direct resistance.

I've been down this road myself in the early days of my career, especially when I lacked a solid track record. Clients would propose, "Can I pay you later when I see results?" or even the audacious "Can you work for free?" Now, let's explore a couple of ways to handle such objections.

1. Metaphors and Questions:

One effective strategy involves crafting a metaphor to paint a vivid picture in the prospect's mind. For instance, compare your services to buying a Porsche. Ask the prospect to imagine walking into a Porsche dealership, expressing the desire to take the car home for a month before deciding to pay. This metaphorical scenario prompts the prospect to consider the absurdity of the request.

Alternatively, liken the situation to dining at a restaurant. Pose the question: "Can you walk up to the restaurant owner and say, 'I'll eat the meal, evaluate it at home, and decide later if I want to pay'?" These metaphors subtly convey the value of your time and expertise.

2. Sarcastic yet Respectful Responses:

Another approach involves responding with a touch of sarcasm, mixed with respect. A straightforward yet slightly humorous retort can convey the message that you are a professional who values your time. For instance, draw a parallel between your work and other professional services. Pose the question: "Could you walk into a restaurant, have a meal, then decide if you want to pay after evaluating your bathroom experience?"

Remember, your tonality and mindset play a crucial role in these responses. Approaching the situation with confidence, conviction, and a firm understanding of your worth reinforces your position and communicates to the prospect that you are a professional deserving of compensation.

While there might be instances where pro bono work is acceptable for gaining experience, this chapter emphasizes the importance of closing deals and securing payment for your services. It's about setting the tone, knowing your value, and confidently navigating the sales conversation. With finesse, objection handling becomes an art form—a dance that propels you closer to a successful close.

Handling the request for free work is a delicate situation in any professional context. It's essential to maintain the value of your services while navigating the conversation diplomatically. Here are some effective responses to address the request:

Clarify Your Value: Politely remind the client of the value and expertise you bring to the table. Emphasize the quality of your work and the positive impact it can have on their goals.

Example:

"I appreciate your interest in my services. My work is crafted with attention to detail and is tailored to meet your specific needs. While I don't provide free services, I'm confident that the value you'll receive will far exceed the investment."

Offer a Limited Scope: If appropriate, consider offering a limited scope of work as a demonstration of your capabilities. This could be a small task or a consultation that showcases your skills without compromising the value of your services.

Example:

"I understand your budget considerations. While I can't provide full services for free, I'm open to discussing a limited scope or a consultation to demonstrate how I can contribute to your project."

Highlight Past Successes: Share success stories or examples of how your services have positively impacted other clients. This helps build credibility and reinforces the idea that your work brings tangible results.

Example:

"I completely understand the need to assess the value of my services. In the past, clients who invested in my work saw significant improvements in [specific outcomes]. I believe we can achieve similar success for your project."

Propose a Trial Period: Suggest a trial period or a pilot project at a reduced rate. This allows the client to experience your work without committing to the full cost upfront.

Example:

"To ensure you're comfortable with my services, how about we start with a trial period at a reduced rate? This way, you can assess the value I bring to your project before making a larger commitment."

Express Understanding and Educate: Acknowledge their budget constraints and take the opportunity to educate them on the investment required for quality work. Help them understand the long-term benefits of investing in professional services.

Example:

"I understand budget considerations are crucial. It might be helpful to discuss the long-term benefits of investing in professional services. Quality work often leads to greater efficiency, better results, and ultimately, a higher return on investment."

Set Boundaries: Politely but firmly communicate your policies regarding free work. Be transparent about your commitment to delivering high-quality services and the resources required to do so.

Example:

"While I can't provide services for free, I'm committed to delivering exceptional results that will add significant value to your project. I have certain policies in place to ensure the quality of my work, and I'd be happy to discuss those with you."

Remember to maintain a professional and respectful tone throughout the conversation. By asserting the value of your services and offering alternative solutions, you can address the client's request without compromising your worth as a professional.

CHAPTER NINETEEN

Mastering the Art of Follow-Up: A Subtle Dance of Value

The post-sales call phase can be a delicate dance, especially when met with responses like "I want to think about it" or "I need to talk to my business partner." Navigating the follow-up without appearing too aggressive or salesy is an art in itself. In this chapter, we'll unravel the strategies to master the subtle dance of follow-up, ensuring your prospects feel valued without feeling pressured.

Understanding the Initial Objection:

Firstly, it's crucial to dissect the initial objection. Whether it's the need for time, discussions with a partner, budget constraints, or any other reason, it's important to recognize that prospects might not always be completely transparent. They might provide polite objections to avoid confrontation, hurting feelings, or admitting a lack of budget.

Effective follow-up stems from a thorough understanding of the prospect's true objections, obtained during the initial conversation. This involves meticulous note-taking and a commitment to extract the real reasons behind their hesitations.

Eliminating Time-wasters:

Not all prospects are worth pursuing. If, after proper qualification, it's clear that a prospect lacks the desire, ability, or trust to make a purchase, it's essential not to waste time. Efficient sales professionals identify and eliminate such prospects early on, redirecting their efforts toward more promising opportunities.

Follow-Up Frequency:

One of the pitfalls in follow-up is finding the right balance between being forgotten and appearing overly eager. The ideal follow-up frequency varies based on factors such as transaction size, the nature of the product or service, and the prospect's buying cycle. Implementing a sensible follow-up schedule in your CRM system ensures consistency without becoming a nuisance.

The Value-Centric Approach:

The key to a successful follow-up is to focus on delivering value consistently. Instead of bombarding prospects with desperate messages like, "Are you ready to buy now?" or "Do you want to do business yet?"—which can come across as pushy and needy—you shift the conversation.

Follow up with valuable content that is personalized to their needs. If a prospect's pain point is lead generation, provide them with insightful articles, podcasts, or videos addressing effective lead generation strategies. Each touchpoint serves as an opportunity to subtly inquire about their progress without pressuring them into a decision.

Positioning as a Trusted Advisor:

Maintain the posture of a trusted advisor rather than an eager salesperson. Your role is to solve their problems, and this should resonate in every interaction. Instead of explicitly asking if they're ready to buy, inquire about their challenges, subtly checking if the issues you discussed previously have seen improvement.

Unexpected Outcomes:

Strangely, the more you focus on providing value without the overt intention of closing, the more likely prospects are to contact you when they're ready. This patient and value-centric approach can lead to unexpected outcomes, such as prospects reaching out to initiate business discussions.

In some cases, prospects may realize they're not the right fit for your solution, but your helpfulness prompts them to refer your services to others. This underscores the importance of building relationships and trust even in scenarios where an immediate sale isn't guaranteed.

Appealing to Self-Interest:

Fundamentally, every follow-up action must appeal to the prospect's self-interest. By consistently providing value and being genuinely interested in their challenges, you position yourself as a problem solver. This approach builds a foundation of trust, making prospects more likely to engage with you when they're ready to make a decision.

Mastering the art of follow-up involves a delicate balance between persistence and patience, assertiveness and subtlety. By prioritizing the prospect's needs, consistently delivering value, and maintaining the role of a trusted advisor, you'll find yourself leading a dance that seamlessly transitions from objection to close.

Following up with clients who have shown initial disinterest requires a delicate approach to rekindle their attention and potentially turn the situation around. Here are some strategies for following up with clients who are not interested:

Acknowledge Their Decision: Begin by acknowledging their previous decision without dwelling on it. This shows respect for their initial response and sets the stage for a constructive follow-up.

Example:

"I appreciate your earlier response, and I understand that [product/ service] may not have been the right fit at that time."

Provide Additional Information: Offer additional information or updates that might address any concerns they had or provide new insights about your product or service.

Example:

"Since our last conversation, there have been some updates on [specific feature/benefit] that I believe could address the concerns you mentioned. Would you be open to exploring these changes together?"

Highlight New Developments: If there have been positive developments, such as new features, improvements, or success stories from other clients, share this information to rekindle their interest.

Example:

"I wanted to update you on some exciting developments we've had recently, particularly in [specific area]. I believe these changes might make a significant difference for your [company/project]."

Seek Feedback: Politely ask for feedback on why they were not interested initially. This information can provide valuable insights and help tailor your approach in the follow-up.

Example:

"I respect your decision, and I'm curious to understand if there were specific aspects that didn't align with your needs. Your feedback would be incredibly valuable as we continually strive to improve."

Propose Alternatives: Offer alternative solutions or modifications to your proposal that might better align with their requirements or address any concerns they raised.

Example:

"I understand that our previous proposal might not have been a perfect match. I'm open to exploring alternative solutions that better suit your needs. Could we discuss any specific adjustments you'd find beneficial?"

Reiterate Value Proposition: Remind them of the unique value your product or service brings and how it can positively impact their goals. Emphasize key benefits that may not have been fully explored in the initial conversation.

Example:

"While I respect your initial decision, I want to reiterate how our [product/service] has proven beneficial for companies facing similar challenges. The unique value we bring might be worth another consideration."

Offer a No-Pressure Follow-Up: Reassure them that the follow-up is not meant to pressure them into a decision but rather to explore any changes in their situation or needs.

Example:

"I completely understand that circumstances can change. This follow-up is not intended to pressure you but rather to check in and see if there have been any shifts in your priorities or if there's anything new we can assist with."

Set a Future Touchpoint: If the prospect is still not interested, set a future touchpoint or follow-up date. This keeps the door open for potential reevaluation without being overly persistent.

Example:

"I appreciate your time, and I won't be a bother. Would it be alright if I check in with you in a few months to see if anything has changed on your end?"

Remember, persistence should be balanced with respect for their decision. It's crucial to maintain professionalism and create an atmosphere where the client feels comfortable revisiting the conversation at their own pace.

CHAPTER TWENTY

Elevate Your Appointment Game: A Script for the Busy Professional

In the world of B2B sales, securing appointments with busy executives requires finesse and a strategic approach. The typical response of appearing overly flexible or desperate can undermine your credibility. In this chapter, we delve into a powerful script designed to level the playing field, address objections, and confidently secure an appointment.

Acknowledging the Busy Professional:

When met with the objection, "I don't have time to meet with you," it's crucial to establish parity. Acknowledge their busyness while presenting yourself as a fellow professional. By saying, "I understand that you are too busy to meet with me because I am busy also," you communicate professionalism and equal footing.

Addressing the Elephant in the Room:

The script then navigates to the core objection: their doubt about the value you can provide during the appointment. By addressing this concern directly with, "Maybe you're saying that because you're not so sure if I could provide enough value during our appointment for you to take time away from your busy schedule," you showcase empathy and an understanding of their perspective.

Certainty in Value Delivery:

The key pivot comes with a strong assurance that you won't waste their time. Clearly stating, "I'm not gonna ask you to invest time with me unless I know I can ask you several questions to help you clarify your core goals," demonstrates that your intent is to provide tangible value. This builds confidence and addresses the prospect's fear of time-wasting.

The Call to Action:

Closing the script with a firm call to action adds the final touch. "What does Tuesday at 2 PM look like?" positions you as someone who values time and is ready to move forward. This call to action is both specific and assertive, avoiding the common pitfall of appearing unsure or overly accommodating.

Tonality Matters:

While the script provides a solid structure, the delivery is equally important. Practicing with the right tonality ensures that the script comes across as confident and genuine rather than rehearsed. Confidence, empathy, and a genuine desire to add value should shine through in every word.

Addressing the objection of not having time to meet requires a thoughtful and considerate response. Here are some strategies to navigate this objection effectively:

Acknowledge and Empathize: Start by acknowledging the prospect's busy schedule and expressing empathy for their time constraints. This shows understanding and validates their current situation.

Example:

"I completely understand that your schedule is incredibly busy, and your time is valuable. I appreciate you letting me know."

Propose a Shorter Meeting: Suggest a shorter, more concise meeting to accommodate their busy schedule. Assure them that you respect their time and can tailor the discussion to fit within a specified timeframe.

Example:

"I completely respect your time commitments. How about we schedule a brief, focused meeting for 15-20 minutes to discuss the most important aspects that directly impact your needs?"

Highlight the Benefits of the Meeting: Emphasize the value and potential benefits they could gain from the meeting. Clearly communicate how the discussion can address their specific challenges or goals.

Example:

"While I understand your time constraints, I believe a brief meeting could provide valuable insights into [specific benefit or solution]. It's an opportunity to explore how we can tailor our approach to meet your unique needs."

Offer Flexible Meeting Options: Provide flexible meeting options, such as virtual meetings or conference calls, to make it more convenient for the prospect. This shows your willingness to adapt to their preferred mode of communication.

Example:

"If an in-person meeting is challenging right now, I completely understand. We can also arrange a virtual meeting or a conference call at a time that suits you best. What would be more convenient for you?"

Share an Agenda in Advance: Provide a clear agenda for the meeting in advance. This allows the prospect to see the specific topics that will be covered and reassures them that the discussion will be focused and efficient.

Example:

"To make the most of our time, I've outlined a concise agenda for our meeting. This way, we can address your key concerns efficiently. Does this agenda align with what you'd like to discuss?"

Highlight Success Stories: Share success stories or examples of how similar meetings with your clients have resulted in positive outcomes. This can build confidence in the value of the discussion.

Example:

"I understand time is tight. Many of our clients initially felt the same way, but after a focused meeting, they discovered solutions that significantly impacted their [specific area]. I believe a similar discussion could be beneficial for you."

Propose Alternative Communication Methods: If an immediate meeting is not possible, suggest alternative communication methods such as email or a brief phone call to address specific questions or concerns.

Example:

"I completely respect your schedule. If a meeting is challenging right now, perhaps we could address your specific questions or concerns through a brief phone call or email exchange. What works best for you?"

Be Flexible with Timing: Offer flexibility in scheduling the meeting, allowing the prospect to choose a time that aligns with their availability. This puts them in control of the timing.

Example:

"I understand your schedule is packed. Would it be helpful if I provided a few time slots, and you could choose the one that works best for you? I want to ensure our discussion is at a time that suits you."

Remember to adapt these responses based on the specific context of your interaction and the nature of your business. The key is to show understanding, flexibility, and a genuine commitment to respecting the prospect's time constraints.

CHAPTER TWENTY-ONE

Mastering the Art of Guarantee: Turning Objections into Commitments

In the world of sales, the dreaded question about guarantees can make or break a deal. This chapter provides a strategic approach to handling the guarantee objection and turning it into a powerful commitment. Before diving into the exact line to use, let's explore three key lessons to ensure you navigate this objection with finesse.

Lesson 1: Do Not Assume

When faced with the guarantee objection, resist the urge to assume the prospect's intention. Don't jump to conclusions or overexplain your guarantee policies. Sometimes, the prospect is merely curious. Stay calm and professional, treating the objection as an inquiry rather than a deal-breaker.

Lesson 2: Don't Take Things Literally

Avoid taking objections at face value. Instead of a direct response, turn the question back to the prospect. Respond with a question like, "Exactly what kind of guarantee are you looking for?" This not only prevents assumptions but also provides clarity on their specific concerns.

Lesson 3: Do Not Justify

Refrain from going into justification mode. Don't launch into a lengthy explanation of your guarantee policies. Instead, qualify the prospect by understanding the motive behind their question. By doing so, you can discern whether their concern is genuine or a smokescreen for a different objection.

Turning Objections into Commitments: The Art of Preemption

Now, armed with these lessons, let's explore the script for handling the guarantee objection.

Prospect: "Well, do you have any kind of guarantee?"

Sales Professional: "Suppose we offer some kind of guarantee. What would that look like for you?"

By turning the objection into a question, you avoid assumptions and gain insight into the prospect's specific expectations. This approach helps you tailor your response to their unique concerns.

If the prospect provides a specific scenario, such as wanting a guarantee tied to revenue growth, continue to turn the conversation into a commitment. For instance:

Prospect: "I want a guarantee that my revenue will increase by 300% in 30 days."

Sales Professional: "Hypothetically, if we could offer that, what's the next step for you?"

This method puts the prospect in a commitment mindset, revealing their true intentions. It also allows you to steer the conversation towards realistic expectations and uncover the prospect's genuine needs.

The Power of Preemptive Selling

The chapter concludes by emphasizing the importance of preemptive selling. Instead of reactive objection handling, take a proactive approach by addressing concerns before they arise. By doing so, you shift from a defensive stance to an offensive one, paving the way for smoother, commitment-driven sales interactions.

Addressing a client's inquiry about guarantees is an important aspect of building trust and confidence in your product or service. Here are effective ways to respond when clients ask, "Do you have a guarantee?"

Express Confidence: Start by expressing your confidence in the value and effectiveness of your product or service. This sets a positive tone and reinforces your belief in what you offer.

Example:

"Absolutely, we stand behind the quality of our [product/service]. I'm confident that you'll find it to be [describe a key benefit or advantage]."

Highlight Key Benefits: Emphasize the key benefits or features that make your product or service stand out. This helps to indirectly address their concerns by showcasing the value they can expect.

Example:

"While we don't have a traditional guarantee, what sets us apart is [highlight a unique feature or benefit]. This ensures that our customers consistently experience [positive outcome]."

Clarify Expectations: Clearly communicate what clients can expect in terms of results, service, or support. Managing expectations upfront helps to build trust and transparency.

Example:

"While we don't offer a specific guarantee, I can assure you that our team is dedicated to [provide a specific aspect of service]. This ensures that you'll receive [desired outcome]."

Offer Trial Period or Demo: If applicable, suggest a trial period or a demo to allow clients to experience your product or service before making a commitment. This reduces their perceived risk.

Example:

"To give you complete confidence in our offering, we can arrange a trial period or a demo. This way, you can experience firsthand how our [product/service] meets your expectations."

Share Customer Success Stories: Provide real-life examples of satisfied customers who have benefited from your product or service. This builds credibility and demonstrates the positive experiences others have had.

Example:

"While we don't have a formal guarantee, many of our customers have achieved [specific results]. Let me share a few success stories that highlight the impact of our [product/service]."

Flexible Refund or Return Policy: If applicable, communicate a flexible refund or return policy. Assure clients that if they are not satisfied, there are mechanisms in place to address their concerns.

Example:

"While we don't have a traditional guarantee, we do have a flexible return policy. If, for any reason, you're not satisfied, we'll work with you to find a solution that meets your expectations."

Educate on Value-Based Guarantees: Educate clients on the concept of value-based guarantees, emphasizing that your commitment is to deliver value and exceed their expectations.

Example:

"While we may not have a standard guarantee, our commitment is to provide exceptional value. Our goal is to exceed your expectations and ensure your complete satisfaction with our [product/service]."

Invite Questions and Discussion: Encourage clients to ask any specific questions or express any concerns they may have. This creates an open dialogue and allows you to address their individual needs.

Example:

"I appreciate your question. Is there anything specific you're concerned about or any particular aspect you'd like more information on? I'm here to address any questions you may have."

Remember to tailor your response based on the nature of your product or service and the specific concerns raised by the client. The key is to instill confidence and provide reassurance through clear communication and a customer-centric approach.

CHAPTER TWENTY-TWO

Navigating the Research Landscape: Guiding Clients through Informed Decision-Making

Introduction:

In the ever-evolving landscape of business, clients often find themselves standing at the crossroads of decisions, armed with the desire to delve into research before making informed choices. Recognizing the pivotal role effective guidance plays in this research journey, businesses are exploring comprehensive strategies to engage clients and offer support throughout the decision-making process. This article explores key strategies that not only facilitate the research process but also contribute to a more enriched and client-centric experience.

Facilitating the Research Process

Acknowledging a client's need for research is the first step toward building a strong foundation for engagement. By offering assistance in gathering necessary information, businesses can demonstrate their commitment to a client's decision-making process. This might involve providing additional materials, relevant case studies, or connecting clients with valuable resources that can aid in their research.

Example: "Absolutely, I understand the importance of thorough research. To assist you in the process, I can provide additional materials, case studies, or connect you with relevant resources. What specific information would be most helpful for your research?"

Highlighting Unique Selling Points

In the sea of options, reminding clients of the unique selling points of your product or service is crucial. Take this opportunity to reemphasize key features or benefits that set your offering apart from alternatives. Reinforcing these points keeps your business top of mind as clients navigate through their research.

Example: "I completely support your decision to research. In the meantime, let me highlight a few unique aspects of our [product/service] that you might find interesting. These are key factors that often resonate with our clients."

Sharing Customer Testimonials

Real-world experiences from satisfied customers can be powerful tools in influencing decisions. Providing testimonials offers a glimpse into the positive experiences others have had with your product or service, adding a human touch to the decision-making process.

Example: "I understand the importance of research. In the meantime, here are testimonials from clients who were once in a similar position. Hearing about their experiences might provide valuable insights for your research."

Scheduling a Follow-Up Meeting

Rather than letting the conversation end at the mention of research, proactive businesses propose scheduling a follow-up meeting. This ensures that any questions or additional information needs can be addressed promptly, maintaining an active and ongoing dialogue.

Example: "I appreciate your commitment to research. How about we schedule a follow-up meeting next week? By then, you might have specific questions or insights from your research that we can discuss in more detail."

Offering to Address Specific Concerns

Encouraging clients to share specific concerns or questions during their research demonstrates a commitment to addressing individual needs. Proactively offering assistance in resolving issues fosters a sense of trust and support.

Example: "I completely understand the need for research. If there are specific aspects or concerns you come across during your exploration, feel free to reach out. I'm here to provide any additional information or clarity you may need."

Providing Additional Resources

To support clients in their research endeavors, businesses can offer additional resources such as whitepapers or case studies that delve deeper into their product or service. This not only showcases transparency but also positions the business as a reliable source of comprehensive information.

Example: "I respect your diligence in research. To support your efforts, I can send over some additional resources that delve deeper into our [product/service]. These documents might offer valuable insights for your decision-making process."

Asking About Their Research Criteria

Tailoring assistance based on the specific criteria or factors clients are considering in their research ensures that businesses provide information that is directly relevant to their decision-making priorities.

Example: "I understand you're conducting research. Can you share the key criteria or factors you're focusing on? This will help me provide you with the most relevant information and insights for your decision-making."

Conclusion:

In the complex landscape of client decision-making, businesses have the opportunity to be more than just providers; they can be trusted guides. By implementing these strategies, businesses can navigate clients through the research maze, offering not just products or services, but a comprehensive and supportive experience that fosters informed decisions and long-term relationships.

CHAPTER TWENTY-THREE

The Value Nexus: A Business Dialogue

In the dynamic realm of sales, the ability to effectively communicate the value proposition of your product or service is a skill that can significantly impact the outcome of a client meeting. This comprehensive guide explores various strategies and examples to reinforce the value proposition, break down the cost versus value, align with the client's budget through customization, highlight long-term benefits, conduct competitive comparisons, offer added value or bonuses, discuss return on investment (ROI), and explore flexible payment options.

1. Value Proposition Reinforcement

"I appreciate your concern about the price. Let me highlight the significant value you'll receive with our [product/service]. Our [specific feature] ensures [benefit], which can have a substantial impact on [client's goal]."

When reinforcing the value proposition, the key is to focus on the unique features and benefits that set your offering apart. Addressing the client's concerns about the price upfront demonstrates transparency and a commitment to delivering real value. Use specific examples to illustrate how your product or service directly contributes to achieving the client's goals.

2. Breakdown of Cost vs. Value

"I understand the importance of considering costs. Let me break down how our pricing correlates with the value you'll receive. For [investment], you gain [specific benefits], which translates to [quantifiable outcome]."

Breaking down the cost versus value involves a strategic examination of the investment in relation to the tangible benefits. Provide a clear and detailed breakdown of the costs, emphasizing the direct correlation to the value delivered. This approach instills confidence in the client by offering a transparent view of the return on their investment.

3. Customization for Budget Alignment

"I hear your concern about the price. Let's explore how we can tailor a package that aligns better with your budget. This way, you still get the essential benefits without exceeding your financial expectations."

Customization for budget alignment is about finding a middle ground that meets both the client's financial constraints and their specific needs. By discussing tailored packages, you demonstrate flexibility and a commitment to delivering value within the client's budgetary parameters.

4. Highlighting Long-Term Benefits

"I understand the upfront cost is a consideration. However, let's look at the long-term benefits. Our [product/service] is an investment that pays off over time, contributing to [client's long-term goal]."

Shifting the focus to long-term benefits involves painting a picture of sustained value. Illustrate how the initial investment transforms into a valuable asset, contributing to the client's overarching, long-term goals. This perspective fosters a forward-looking mindset and positions your offering as an integral part of the client's future success.

5. Competitive Comparison

"I appreciate your concern about pricing. When compared to alternatives, our [product/service] stands out due to [unique features]. While the price might be higher, the added value justifies the investment."

Conducting a competitive comparison involves positioning your offering in the market landscape. Clearly articulate the unique features that set your product or service apart, even if the price is higher than alternatives. Emphasize the added value that justifies the investment, reinforcing the notion that quality surpasses cost.

6. Offering Added Value or Bonuses

"I understand price is a consideration. To make this a more appealing proposition, we can include [bonus feature] at no additional cost. This enhances the overall value you receive with our [product/service]."

Offering added value or bonuses goes beyond the standard product or service. It involves sweetening the deal by providing additional features or perks at no extra cost. This strategy enhances the perceived value, making the overall proposition more appealing to the client.

7. Discussing Return on Investment (ROI)

"I hear your concern about the price. Let's delve into the expected return on investment. With our [product/service], the benefits you'll gain can significantly outweigh the initial cost, providing a strong ROI."

Initiating a conversation about the return on investment is about showcasing the long-term value your offering brings. Illustrate how the benefits and outcomes extend far beyond the initial cost, emphasizing a strong return on investment. This approach aligns with the client's desire for a strategic and lucrative partnership.

8. Exploring Flexible Payment Options

"I understand the price might be a stretch. We can explore flexible payment options that suit your budget. This way, you can still enjoy the full benefits of our [product/service]."

Exploring flexible payment options is a practical strategy to address immediate financial concerns. By providing alternatives such as installment plans or financing, you ease the client's immediate burden, making the investment more manageable and accessible.

In conclusion, mastering the art of value communication in sales involves a holistic approach that addresses various aspects of client concerns. By reinforcing the value proposition, breaking down costs, customizing for budget alignment, highlighting long-term benefits, conducting competitive comparisons, offering added value, discussing ROI, and exploring flexible payment options, you position your offering as not just a product or service but a strategic investment in the client's success. These strategies, when executed effectively, create a compelling narrative that resonates with clients and fosters long-term, mutually beneficial relationships.

CHAPTER TWENTY-FOUR

Striking the Balance: Professionalism and Personal Connection in Sales

In the intricate dance of sales, the question of whether you should be friends with your customer is a nuanced one, demanding careful consideration of boundaries, professionalism, and the unique dynamics of each relationship. This chapter explores the delicate balance between cultivating a friendly rapport and maintaining a professional demeanor in the world of sales.

Understanding the Boundaries:

Professional Boundaries:

While a friendly rapport is beneficial, it's crucial to maintain professional boundaries. The customer-salesperson relationship is rooted in mutual respect and a shared objective: meeting the customer's needs. Straying into overly personal territory can blur these professional lines.

Example: Imagine you discover through casual conversation that your customer shares a hobby with you, such as golf. It's acceptable to briefly acknowledge this shared interest, but delving too deep into personal matters, like family issues or unrelated personal challenges, may cross the line into unprofessional territory.

How Much Should You Know?

Relevant Information:

Knowing your customer on a personal level doesn't mean delving into every aspect of their life. Focus on relevant information that aids in understanding their needs, preferences, and challenges related to the product or service you provide.

Example: If you're selling software solutions to a marketing team, understanding their team dynamics, preferred communication styles, and key pain points related to marketing software is pertinent. However, details about their personal life, unless willingly shared, may not contribute significantly to the business relationship.

Navigating Humor and Jokes:

Shared Laughter:

Humor can be a powerful tool to build rapport, but it should be approached with sensitivity. Shared laughter can create a positive atmosphere, but jokes should be light, non-controversial, and considerate of diverse perspectives.

Example: During a casual conversation, if a customer makes a light-hearted joke about the challenges of their industry, responding with a similarly light and industry-related joke can contribute to a friendly atmosphere. Avoid humor that may be divisive, offensive, or unrelated to the business context.

Social Interactions Outside Business:

Lunches and Events:

Occasional social interactions, such as lunches or industry events, can strengthen your relationship. However, these interactions should remain professional, with a focus on discussing business-related topics.

Example: Inviting a customer to a business lunch to discuss upcoming projects or industry trends is appropriate. However, inviting them to a purely social event, like a family barbecue or personal celebration, may blur the lines between personal and professional boundaries.

Striking the Right Balance:

Tailoring to Individual Preferences:

The comfort level with friendliness varies among customers. Some may appreciate a more casual rapport, while others prefer a strictly professional interaction. Tailor your approach based on the cues and preferences of each individual customer.

Example: If a customer consistently steers conversations toward business matters and avoids personal anecdotes, respect their preference for a more formal interaction. Conversely, if a customer engages in casual conversation, reciprocating with friendly banter can enhance your rapport.

In the realm of sales, the key is to strike a balance that nurtures relationships without compromising professionalism. Being friendly with your customer is not about becoming their confidant; rather, it's about creating a positive and respectful atmosphere that enhances collaboration. By navigating the nuances of personal connection with finesse, you can cultivate strong, enduring relationships that extend beyond mere transactions.

"Santiago, the shepherd boy, wandered through the ruins of a castle nestled in the Andalusian hills. As he traced the ancient stones with his fingers, he felt a deep resonance within him. The ruins spoke of a time long past, of dreams and ambitions that had once soared within those walls. The shepherd, much like the castle, stood at the threshold of the unknown. His journey, guided by the whispers of the wind and the language of the desert, was a quest to unravel the mysteries of his own heart. The path ahead was uncertain, yet Santiago embraced the wanderer within him, knowing that every step he took was a step toward discovering the treasures that awaited him on the journey, and the alchemy that could transform his wandering into wisdom."
- "The Alchemist" by Paulo Coelho